Becoming Mum

By J.C. D'Ath

2014 *Becoming Mum*

First Edition

ISBN 978-1-312-02974-3

For Aria

baby
sleep
time
feeding
hours
mum
start
think
home
year
changed
wonder
work
life
Husband
Bean
Little
parents
night
good
bottle
formula
love
actually
breastfeeding
myself
thought
people
house
writing
realised
help
born
eat
family
crying
worried
tired
hair
end
long
kids
labour
daughter
happy
milk
person
attempt
guilty
friends
lot
stop
play
dream
possible
words
definitely
hope
ability
smile
guilt
used
read
doctor
remember
mother
care
nurse
incredibly
completely
tell
Yes

Thank You

This book was published with funds collected through crowd sourcing on Pledgeme.co.nz. Without the following people, this book could not have been published, and I am eternally grateful for so many people coming together to help me reach my goal!

Thank you to the Infant pledgers:

Amanda Atlas, Donna Buchanan, Jeff Cloniger, Elly D'Ath, Kathy D'Ath, Katherine Doig, Jo Domigan, Saul Gibney, Maria Gibney, Shirley Gibney, Melinda Goodger, Summer Hebberd, Jess Johnson, Theresa Koorey, Emma Luisa Malou, Clare Mulligan-Hjorring, Gary Thomas, Max Tocker and the mysterious anonymous pledger.

Thank you to the Toddler Pledgers:

Emily Burn and Erin D'Ath

Thank you to the Preschool to Teenager Pledgers:

Elly Bucher, Vincent and Alison D'Ath, and Rebekah Stewart.

Thank you to the incredible Sonya Watson who runs the Mothers Matter PND support group in Christchurch. You work tirelessly for us mums and your work doesn't go unnoticed. You were looking out for me even before I met you or knew whom you were..

Thank you to my family and friends who have supported me throughout everything, from starting this blog in a moment of panic, to getting it published, and all the crazy hormone-fueled episodes in between. Thank you for supporting me and giving me time to write.

Super Special Thank You's

Thank you to my Husband Saul. You are my soul mate and best friend, you understand me when others do not, and together we are on an amazing journey. I wouldn't want to travel this road with anyone else. I love you.

Thank you to my Mum for dealing with all the crazy phone calls and for being my other best friend and incidental therapist on more than your fair share of occasions. You are the best mum ever, I wake up each day hoping I will be as good a mum as you are. I love you so much!

Thank you to everyone who supported me and followed (and continues to follow) my journey via my blog at:

anxietygirlgetspregnant.blogspot.co.nz

It means the world to me.

January 18

The Bun in the Oven

The day I found out I was pregnant the house caught on fire. I had been toasting some super healthy sugar-free muesli in the oven, and I went and peed on a stick while I waited. I counted to 120 and then I saw the second line. Next thing I know, the fire alarm is going off and my Husband is yelling, "You've caught the oven on fire!" I walked into a cloud of smoke beneath the incessant beeping from the alarm, and said dazedly, "I'm pregnant," to which he replied, "That's great but the house is on fire!" I saw flames leaping out of the oven, and thrusting the stick of terror into my Husband's hand, I grabbed the fire extinguisher and proceeded to douse my muesli and the oven in one go.

Flames out. Crisis averted.

But I am still pregnant.

My Husband didn't know what two lines meant. I explained that meant I was pregnant, and I'd never had two lines show up before. He immediately insisted I take another test to make sure. That one also showed up positive. So did the next one. Then he insisted that we needed a more expensive test.

All up, I took a total of four tests that night, and two more the next morning (plus one at the doctors), each one positive. Weirdly enough, the number of positives wasn't helping me accept the fact any more. We had been trying. We wanted a kid. We were totally ready, but I wasn't feeling the anticipated excitement. I was simply feeling downright terrified.

"I can't do it!" I declared later that evening. "There's simply no way I'm going to cope!" Thoughts of vomit, pain and public humiliation crowded my head. Ongoing discomfort and horrendous labour were all I could think about. "You'll be fine, remember we wanted a baby," counseled my Husband.

"I want the baby," I clarified, then added, "But can we get someone else to do the pregnancy bit?"

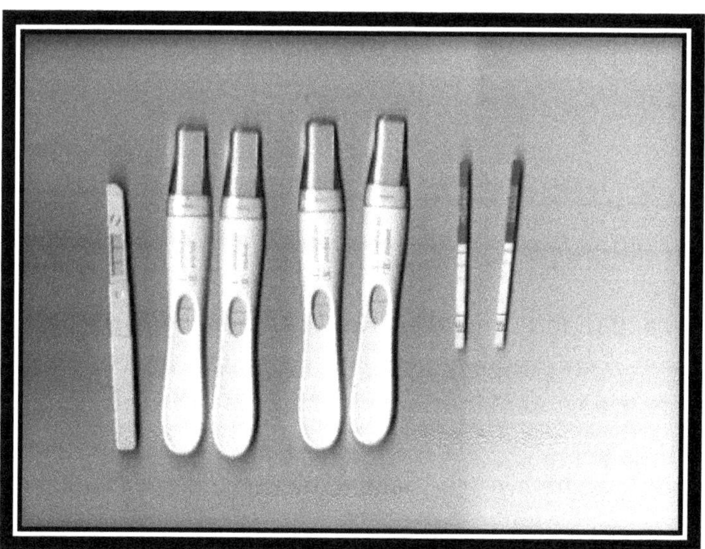

Jan 21

BABYDUST!

Apparently being pregnant now requires you to learn a new language.

I admit, I have become a serial troller of Google forums and pregnancy sites in an effort to understand what the hell is happening to me. Is this weird sensation normal? Has anyone else had this too??

But they aren't very helpful, and not just because it seems that the range of sensations is huge and varied, but because I honestly cannot understand what is being said.

For instance: "My DH and I have been TTC for 4 months now. When we TTC my DD and DS I got a BFP at 11 DPO. I'm 14 DPO and haven't got AF yet but I did a HPT with my FMU, and got a BFN. Does this mean I'm not PG??"

WHAT THE F* $K DOES THAT MEAN???!

Well, dear reader, apparently it means this.

Translation: "My dear Husband and I have been trying to conceive for 4 months now. When we tried to conceive my darling daughter and darling son, I got a big fat positive at 11 days post ovulation. I'm 14 days post ovulation and haven't got Aunt Flow yet, but I did a home pregnancy test with my first morning urine and got a big fat negative. Does this mean I'm not pregnant??"

Dear God!

It's an entire secret language that must be learnt by all who enter this weird and mysterious world of the pregnant.

I mean, OMG, WTF! This post is so OTT and contains TMI for the DH to handle. TBH since I didn't get AF and got 5 BFP, I'm really looking forward to being a SAHM, and even a WAHM. LOL. Anyway,

JTYLTK, BABYDUST!

Feb 14

Relapse

Three weeks ago, I found out that I was pregnant. Now, this is a great thing, don't get me wrong. But that doesn't change the fact, that I am simply terrified!

The day before I found out, I was discharged by my anxiety counselor as I had reached a good place and had plans in place to manage further anxiety and depression, then WHAMMO! Here is something new and scary for you to deal with. Needless to say, my doctor instantly referred me back to her—"the quickest relapse in history," I joked on the phone.

I am dealing with many weird feelings that I can't control. On the one hand, I am extremely excited to be a mum. On the other hand, I am pretty convinced that I am going to be in a state of panic for most of the pregnancy, and won't be able to cope. I am afraid of what my medications will do to the baby, I am afraid that I can't cope with morning sickness, that I will be anxious non-stop for nine months, that I will be the one woman in the history of the planet who cannot physically manage being pregnant, let alone the labour at the end.

In short, I want to be knocked out now, and woken up when it's over.

But what am I even worried about? Pregnancy is a joyous time, with glowing skin and happy anticipation. Everyone congratulates you and comments on how happy you must be. I smile and agree, but on the inside I am crumbling amidst the knowledge that I have lost control of my body for the meantime, that waves of nausea will hit me without notice, that I am sore, and tired and hungry and generally just afraid. But I don't mention any of this, because then I sound like a bad mum-to-be.

Feb 17

Food, Glorious Food

Cravings are real. And they SUCK if what you are craving is not within easy 'getting' distance.

So far, I've craved:

1. **Chicken Pie** - when my Husband told me he was going to make it for tea...I cried. Literally. Then I cried again the next day when he told me we didn't have enough ingredients to make it the following night.

2. **Burger King Whopper** - haven't had one in YEARS, took my Husband one hour to get one for me in peak traffic.

3. **Teriyaki Udon Noodles** - finally got the ingredients and made this myself after thinking about it for over a week.

4. **Ice Cream with tinned peaches** - threw a major hormonal tantrum at poor Husband after he got it from the supermarket, then *failed* (FAILED I TELL YOU) to actually put it in a bowl and serve it to me.

Sigh. At least I am not craving chalk...

March 6

To Show, or Not to Show?

One week away from our first proper scan, and people are already asking whether I'm 'keeping a secret from them', giving me eating advice, and suggesting what type of shirts I should wear. This does not bode well. To be honest, this has been a terribly kept secret from the start, but is it possible to be showing at just 11 weeks? I Googled it, WebMDed it, and searched the Huggies forums, but no one had an answer. I don't think I am showing, I'm pretty sure I've just got fat.

To make it worse, I am craving pies....and WINE!!—seriously, how is that fair? Obviously I am not drinking the wine, but the pie craving is slightly overwhelming. I clearly don't stand a chance of coming out of this pregnancy with any semblance of my former self. But is that the point? Before I got pregnant, one of my main reasons for not getting pregnant was a paralysing fear of labour. Now, I'm excited about it because it will mean that this whole pregnancy business is OVER!

March 13

Day Before the Scan

One day until the big scan. So many questions and worries running round my head. Will they say, "There's nothing there, you're imagining it, you're just fat." Or worse, "I'm sorry to tell you, but your baby is dead." But it's true that I'm fat, at 12 weeks apparently I already look pregnant. At least, enough so that my students feel ok to ask me outright, "Miss, are you pregnant?" And friends are telling me that people are asking them if I am, because I look like I'm showing. When that happened before I would cry, be offended. It doesn't matter that that wasn't what they intended, at least most of the time.

What if I'm told, "It's twins, no wait triplets..." How could I possibly cope with more than one!

My skin is 14 years old again and wouldn't you know it, I can't use Proactiv. Who knew that skin care products could harm your baby. Just one more item to add to the already massive list of things to avoid. Soft eggs, raw eggs, soft cheese, processed meats, alcohol, cold chicken, hot baths, saunas, hummus, pate, soft serve ice cream, mayonnaise, food from cabinets, reheated foods, buffet foods, unpasteurised foods, salads, cold pasta! When I add the list of things that now make we want to vomit (fried foods, stir-fries, noodles, whole steaks (cut up ones are fine?) , what, realistically, is left?

I am living in an anxiety-ridden bubble. Floating between

excitement for the end product and terror of everything that could go wrong. Panicking at every new sensation (and there are many), yet concerned that I've harmed Bub already. Worried that I'm going to get inundated with visitors in September, and afraid that I won't get visited by anyone at all. Anxious that I will have to fly up with Baby to meet the family, stressed that I wont be able to do it and finally, worried that I will not be able to stay sane enough to be a good mum. Let's see what tomorrow's scan will tell us.

March 16

Little Bouncy Hamster

The scan, in short, was amazing. I was so nervous I couldn't eat much breakfast at all. Then I was struggling to drink the amount of water required to inflate my bladder in order to push the uterus into a position where they could see it. So by the time we arrived—a whole half hour early—I was pretty sure they weren't going to see anything (even if there was something to see), and it would be all my fault.

However, luck was in our favour! The 8 am appointment never showed up, so at 8:10 we were ushered down a series of maze-like corridors into a darkened room with a giant screen on the wall. First thing I did? I looked around to see what I could possible throw up into should I get to that point. I lay down, exposed my tummy, and closed my eyes. Determined that if there was something wrong, I didn't want to see it. I just wanted to be let down gently. My Husband gasped and said, "Oh wow," and my eyes were open. There it was. A teeny, tiny human creature larger than life on the screen before us. We certainly didn't need training in radiography to be able to tell for ourselves, there was definitely a baby in there. Not going to lie, there were tears from both of us. Laughter too as we watched baby jumping on the walls of my uterus as though it were a trampoline. The radiographer was having a hard time trying to capture the images needed, as the little monkey kept twisting and turning. Two arms, two hands, ten fingers, two legs and feet, a head, and a tiny beating heart. Everything was just where it should be. At one point it rolled over and faced us, showing us its terrifyingly alien-like face at which we all cried, "Roll back baby!"

After all the stress of the first 12 weeks, it's amazing to finally have a picture. To know it's real. To know that I haven't eaten something bad or taken a too hot bath and ruined it all somehow. Husband is now finally letting himself be excited too. We can finally start looking at baby furniture and other cute things—and we finally let the Facebook universe know! I am not anxious right now. Just very, very excited. I'm even starting to feel ok about the prospect of labour, as that means I will finally get to meet the Little Bean.

Facebook Announcement Fun

March 19

Hands Off!

Just a note. No woman I have ever met likes having her tummy touched. Not by family, not by friends, and certainly not by strangers! I don't know why this changes for some women when they are pregnant, but it hasn't changed for me! Besides, at just about 13 weeks, I am somewhat offended that I am 'showing' at all. I've spent years trying to hide my tummy, to get rid of it, to dress it up so it's disguised, and now what? I'm supposed to just be ok with it? Just like that?! I don't think so. I may well be in denial, but I don't think the belly I currently have is a baby bump. It's certainly not 'cute' as people are suddenly claiming. Pretty sure it's just a result of having to constantly eat to avoid throwing up. So telling me I am showing already feels pretty much the same as it did when people asked if I was pregnant BEFORE I was pregnant. Basically, I need a t-shirt that says, "Yes. I'm Pregnant. No. You cannot touch it!" SMILE! BREATHE! Quickly move on!

March 22

What Were We Thinking?

A sharp, very confident rap on the door awoke us this morning at the ungodly pre-baby Saturday morning time of 8am. A courier. With a parcel! From.....China??

Once I managed to break into the box, we were rather amazed to find a baby monitor (complete with night vision, LCD screen, wireless capabilities and two way intercom system), along with a baby Doppler 'heart-beat-listener-thingy'.

But who on earth sent them? We certainly didn't know the Chinese name listed on the customs ticket, nor had we ordered anything from anywhere at all. A little bit of sleuthing followed, mostly with the clues—who knows me by my married name, and who loves gadgets? In this brilliant day of the Internet, the mysterious present givers were uncovered in a matter of minutes. Thank you, wonderful honorary grandparents, what a great start to the day!

Unfortunately, that's where it ended.

Having been paid this week, I was super excited to go shoe shopping for my rapidly growing feet, as well as potentially decking out the baby room. Yep, in my head, it was going to be that fast, and that simple. I should have learnt that lesson by now, shopping has never been, and never will be, something I am good at.

I got the shoes (and this GREAT pair of bug slippers which will no doubt ensure I am taken seriously at all times) with little problem, and then proceeded to the giant Babycity store.

OH. GOOD. LORD!

Where on earth do you start. Cots are not just cots. They have levels, colours, ratings, different features, brands, some have mobiles attached, some convert into toddler beds, some have extensions, others have 'sleigh' ends. Car seats...don't even get me started. I stood staring at the wall in a somewhat disorientated daze. Do we need a capsule, a convertible car seat, a seat with a three-point harness, one that reclines? Do we need to be able to clip it into a travel thing, or are we after something we can remove from the car? Bottles, breast pumps, breast pads, diaper disposals and cute little brightly coloured feeding utensils swarmed before me in a kaleidoscopic fury. Whilst push chairs, strollers, mountain buggies and convertible strollers with cup holders and iPod chargers (I may have imagined that last one), were all jostling for my attention.

Buy me! You NEED me! Look here! Look there! You will NOT SURVIVE without us! You have NO idea what you are doing!!

Before I walked in, my head was full of cot-buying excitement. Tiny bottles were swirling around my brain, and I could barely contain my excitement at the thought of the cute Peter Rabbit branded blankets we could come out with. But now I was suddenly overwhelmed, intimidated even. I had no idea what I needed, or why I had even thought I could possibly walk into a baby shop at all. Should we be buying anything? How do we know what (if anything) we might be getting as gifts? Suddenly I realised I was hungry. I had to pee (again). Where was my Husband?!

On the way home, I had a wee tantrum in the car, while at the lights, with the window down. Something along the lines of, "Why didn't I listen to myself when we were thinking of having kids? You knew nothing! At least I knew what we were going to be up against. This is awful! I'm so hungry! I already look five months pregnant! I'm going to BE A WHALE!"

The somewhat older than us couple in the next car thought it was hilarious, which then made me laugh, which quickly turned into the first (of three) sets of tears on the way home.

We stopped at McDonalds. Baby wanted a cheeseburger apparently. I bought a Big Mac combo and a cheeseburger, and practically inhaled the cheeseburger. NEVER had a cheeseburger taste so good. Husband laughed at me and offered to drive. But dammit—we were in MY car.

Well, finally we got home, and now I am wearing my bug slippers (oh happy days!), although it is warm. We have decided to have a good look on online auctions—we think we have found a real possible winner of a cot (with all the bedding) that closes in 42 minutes! I should probably get back to being a ninja bidder then!

stopped

March 27

Carried Away on a Tide of Hormones

Yesterday was a bad day. That pretty much sums it up perfectly, but I suppose you readers might need a little more info. Let's start at the top. Firstly, I had a fight with my Husband about going home for Easter weekend and spending the whole time travelling between family's houses. Mainly, he wanted to see his parents, I did not. Clearly, I was not about to compromise.

Secondly, I cried all the way to school, where upon I nearly vomited in front of my students, before proceeding to apologise and run for the exit, only to open the door and set off the library alarms. Cue, much laughter from students, and one bright red, dry-heaving teacher. Not a happy start so far.

But that was just the beginning. Continued to dry-heave every half hour for the next three hours. Then the zip on my last pair of fitting black trousers BROKE. Luckily for me, I was wearing a long top. However I wasn't happy about having to teach a bunch of 13 year olds drama without my pants done up. Thankfully, I am pretty talented, and was able to act like nothing was the matter (and they will NEVER know).

Finally, I drove home, still feeling like I was going to puke. Got home, realised I'd left my wallet AND my drink bottle at school. Climbed into my pyjamas (at 1:30 pm), turned on some very loud, VERY EMOTIONAL music, and proceeded to sing at the top of my choked up, pathetically miserable voice while bawling at the injustice of that certain career in show business that I will now NEVER HAVE THE CHANCE TO FULFILL!

Seriously though—this was meant to be the year where I auditioned for everything and really started giving it a real go to make a career in singing. My Husband is still auditioning and acting and doing fun stuff like that. He's equally as responsible for this baby. So how is that fair?

April 8

Things I Never Expected When I Was Expecting

My anxiety has fluctuated greatly over the past couple of months. One moment I feel fine, like I can handle all these changes and uncertainties like a pro! The next, I look in the mirror, see my spotty skin and growing waistline and freak out. Thoughts like, "I can't do this, get me off!" are not uncommon in our household at those moments. It doesn't help that I feel completely useless next to my superhero Husband who has started doing the groceries, making tea, doing the dishes, the laundry, and still managing to work and rehearse his show, all while I battle the urge to eat an entire box of Coco Pops, struggle to get off the couch, can barely keep my eyes open during the day, yet lay awake all night. Basically, I have become a useless and incompetent incubator who no longer fits anything, nor can walk anywhere for longer than half an hour without having to sit down. I do buy him lots of presents to show him how grateful I am, but it doesn't feel like enough. He says it's fine, but I don't believe it is. I only hope that I can show him how amazing he is and pull through this pregnancy without too many anxious meltdowns!

The top 10 things I never expected when I was expecting (other than how amazing my Husband would be). The 16 weeks edition:

1. My cute tiny feet would grow.

2. My hair would fall out...I thought it was supposed to

stop falling out at all!

3. How quickly I would no longer fit my clothes.

4. How ravenously hungry you can be after eating all day, and how sick being hungry can make you feel.

5. ...I can't quite remember this one......Baby brain! (It's a real thing).

6. That food aversion is just as real as food craving.

7. At the start, it hurts when you cough, it hurts when you sneeze, it hurts when you laugh.

8. Suddenly women everywhere are dying to tell you their pregnancy stories, their birth stories, in fact, any stories.

9. How sore your boobs can get...even going over speed bumps is TORTURE.

10. That I'd stop being so afraid of labour—the thought of not being pregnant is just too good!

And the added bonus thing:

1. How many weird dreams of trying to crawl through tiny spaces I would start having....hmmmm.

2. Did I mention how amazing my Husband would be?

April 15

Remaining Dainty

Remaining dainty whilst pregnant is difficult. Firstly, at 17 weeks, I now feel like I'm about to tip over onto my face, and regularly have to straighten myself up. I feel like I must look somewhat similar to a depressed spotty teenager, or possibly an elderly sloth.

At least, if I could actually reach the ground with my hands anymore, I might look somewhat sloth-like.

Not to mention, that I now cannot stretch up to reach things as I get little pangs in my stretching tummy—this makes writing on the whiteboard rather difficult, in fact, it makes everything difficult, as I am already rather short, so this has essentially shortened me further.

One thing I'm learning this week, being embarrassed and conservative about bodily functions while preggers, is not a good idea. Let it all out they say! (I say...literally?)

Never mind though, we find out the sex in three weeks, and then I can start imagining what fun things I will do to get baby back for this pregnancy debacle.

Imagination starts running down weird tangents involving frightening small children.

Oh little baby, what fun we shall have!

April 22

Attack of the 'What Ifs'!

Yesterday, I treated myself to a pregnancy magazine. Thinking (rather naively as it turns out), that it would make me feel better about all the weird pains, the bad skin, and the impending (and inevitable) labour process. I was wrong.

All the pictures of happy, gorgeous pregnant women did nothing to raise my currently lowered self esteem, nor did the maternity fashion spread, in which the most 'affordable' item of clothing was a tunic (spelt 'tunique') going for $77 AUD. Add to that the article about the three stages of labour in which I read this:

"It is absolutely paramount during labour that you feel 100% safe, as this sets up a colossal chain reaction mentally that can affect your labour physically. Feelings of fear or anger automatically activate our fight and flight hormones such as adrenaline, which quickens the heart rate, tenses muscles, intensifies pain, and during labour, inhibits the synthesis of oxytocin for productive labour contractions. Fear and anger in childbirth become like a strong head wind, hindering progress and lengthening the whole process."

Good. God.

A mild panic attack quickly followed, in which I tried to call my Husband at work. No answer. I had a shower to calm down, but ended up crying instead. Quite simply, I have absolutely no faith in my ability to get through labour without a panic attack. What if I cause the baby distress? What if I make it lose oxygen? What if the midwife yells at me? What if I pass out? What if the doctors think I'm crazy? What if it's my fault something goes wrong? What if.......

Be strong little baby, we will make it through together. Somehow.

April 29

Baby Fashionistas and Knowledgeable Hubbies

Pregnancy magazines are marvelous things, exposing you to the incredible world of (literally) unbelievable baby gadgets. In the magazine I have taken on holiday, there is a baby bath shaped like a sunflower that is soft and fits in your sink. Actually, I think that is pretty cool. Then there is something called a 'Mamaroo', which appears to be nothing more than a space-age bouncinet. You can choose between different 'bounce' functions like 'car ride' (save some petrol), 'kangaroo' (what the...), 'tree swing', 'rock-a-bye' and 'ocean'. Just in case you ever decided the one thing your baby needs is to be carried by a kangaroo, or left to sleep on the ocean. I shouldn't mock it though, I actually really want one...but for $599? I think we need the stroller first.

My Hubby and I just got back from (possibly) our last ever pre-baby holiday. Credit card got a bit of a hit, but nevertheless, it was wonderful! Only thing I am having second thoughts about, is the wisdom I displayed in asking my man to please read the pregnancy mag I bought (see amazing baby gadgets above). It seemed like a great idea at the time, but I forgot that he is a smart, soaker upperer of information (he has four university degrees), and he seems to have memorised the entire magazine. Cue somewhat alarming random comments regarding amniotic fluid (apparently it tastes different depending on what I eat), expressing of milk (if I do this, he can feed the baby at night, not just me...actually, that sounds alright), and his sudden interest in all things crying (he hopes we don't have a colicky baby, don't we all?). I'm beginning to wonder if it weren't better to just let him remain oblivious for the next few months, even if all it meant was that I don't have to think about amniotic fluid in the middle of dinner.

April 30

Baby Brain, It's a Real Thing

Top five baby brain moments so far:

1. Searching for my fuel discount card in my wallet, my bag, my wallet again, under the car seat, wallet again! Oh wait, there it is. In my wallet. Right in the first pocket. Staring right at me.

2. Walking into the supermarket. Carefully recited list of necessaries vanishes inexplicably. Walk up and down aisles for 15 minutes hoping something will come back. Got some stuff. Got back into the car. Drove home. Didn't have what I went there for. Husband not impressed.

3. Walking into a class and prepping the board. Kids I've never seen before walk in for class. Clearly NOT my class. What on earth am I teaching now? Late to class.

4. I really should start writing things down, 'cos number four was a winner.......

5. Is it the first of April or the first of May that's April fools....oh, wait.

May 2

Boy or Girl?

In exactly two hours, we will (hopefully) be told whether we are having a boy, or a girl. I am currently riding a wee emotional rollercoaster, though this morning I was super calm. I drove to the midwife, realised that I'd forgotten my very important maternity folder, turned back for it, realised that would make me 15 minutes late, so turned around again. Chatted happily with my midwife, did the pee test for UTI's, glucose and protein, heard the heartbeat again. It was much louder and stronger this time, so my 'what if' attacks have no grounds at this point, baby is definitely still there. I haven't harmed it with my panic attacks, or having too hot a bath, or lying on my back, side, front, or eating a tiny bit of blue cheese. I also got a medical certificate to verify that I am in fact pregnant, so that I can apply for maternity leave. I left feeling excited and energetic and impatient to get the big scan over with.

A mere hour later I am now on the verge of tears after reading some articles about people giving birth, living with babies, and being pregnant. Not scared tears though, just emotional ones. A lot of things are setting me off lately, it seems it doesn't take much at all. A picture of a cute baby hedgehog, a beautiful song, going to my first pregnancy yoga class, talking to other mums-to-be, and realising that I am normal. I can hardly think straight. I keep forgetting things that shouldn't be so hard to remember. All I can think about is, "is it a girl or a boy?" I'm so excited, I feel like, once we know what sex it is, we can start naming it, and planning properly and that everything will feel even more real than it already is. I don't know why though, as it's already pretty real, and it wouldn't make a difference what we were having, we would still plan the same. But there it is, I have set myself off again!

May 22

THE BIG REVEAL!

IT'S A GIRL! And here is my beautiful little hand. Hello world!

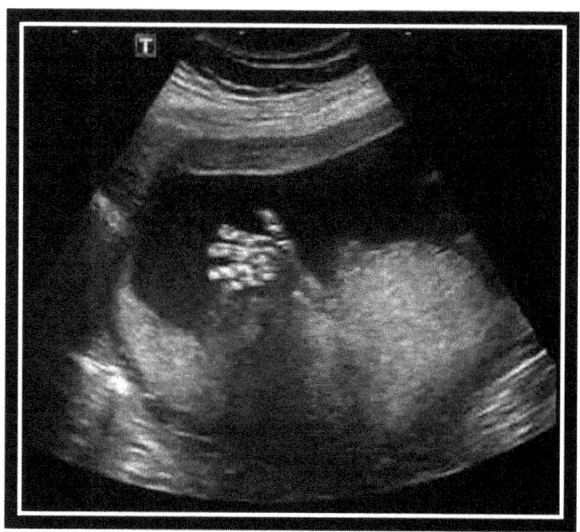

Facebook Announcement Fun Round Two

May 11

Halfway Downsides, Upsides, and Insides

It's official, from now on, my little app counter's 'weeks to go' will be less than 'weeks completed'!! I was told at the start that the second trimester would be the best, that I'd have amazing hair and lots of energy, that I'd be happy and excited and everything would pretty much be like dancing in a crystal lake with singing baby unicorns covered with rainbow swirls flying past.

"NAWWWWWWWWW!"

That was a lie. I am told by the odd person that I am glowing. If that's true, then my body is doing some weird camouflage trick whereby it is hiding the inner ugliness extremely well. I'm not sure what the evolutionary point of this would be, however. For the past couple of months I have been prone to getting very overwhelmed, crying at inappropriate times, and for what seems like very little reason. This isn't the case though—there is a lot on my mind! I am worried about labour, finances, my work situation, my mental state before and after baby gets here. On top of that, there are work, reports, parent interviews, I am putting on a show, a festival and something else probably that I don't even know about! Sigh. At least it's keeping me distracted from the pregnancy a little bit. Baby brain is reaching new, unexplored heights. I am actually a little concerned that I may not remember anything or anyone very soon.

For the past month, I have been losing about three times more hair than normal every time I shower/brush/straighten, or indeed do anything to it in an attempt to feel pretty. This concerns me somewhat, as I was informed that women in fact lost LESS hair while pregnant. In the past week I have been whacked in the face (or esophagus) with the worst heartburn I've ever had! I am now having to sleep in a semi-upright position, which is interesting. Apparently this is because baby is now making its presence really known, and all my insides are getting squished up to make room. Yummy. Yesterday I had my first experience of round ligament pain. That is, short, stabby pains in your lower abdomen. I'm not sure what the point of them is, but they can really make you catch your breath and freeze up. Worst thing is that they happen frequently, and quickly, and over and over again.

On the upside though, we went and bought baby some storage shelves for her room, and also some really bold-coloured storage baskets to fit in the shelves. It looks fantastic, and it was so nice to put some of the things we have collected for her into them rather than leaving them in the cot. And the even better news is I can now sometimes feel the kicks with my hand! I started feeling the movements very, very early, at about 15 weeks. But everyone told me it was highly unlikely, and to be honest, made me feel pretty rubbish about it. But I know now that I WAS feeling kicks, because those little flutters have simply got stronger, and two days ago I put my hand on my bump and felt it move on the outside. It was the best thing ever!

May 15

A Week of Weird

I'm at 21 weeks now, but apparently I am lying about that. I know this, because during this week, four different teachers told me (in a variety of ways) that I looked much further along than I say I am. Some of the best comments:

"You're only 21 weeks? Shouldn't you still be able to hide it?" "You aren't due til September? You look like you've swallowed a basketball!" And a beauty I heard secondhand from students, "Miss is pregnant? I knew it! The rest of the class just thought she was really, really fat." These harmless comments, which were probably forgotten by the perpetrators the instant they uttered them, have been my downfall this week.

On Wednesday morning, I couldn't find a single thing to wear, everything made me look huge, nothing was fitting like it should. I was heading towards a disintegrating meltdown when Husband calmly directed me to, "Go do my teeth," while he endeavored to hunt for my one pair of pregnancy pants. In the end, I went to school in my stretchy gym pants and a t-shirt, cleverly disguised as work pants with a nice jersey. Still, I spent all day worried that I looked enormous, and that every single person was sizing me up. Even today I was asked the wonderful question, "Are you absolutely positive you are not having twins?"

On Tuesday I felt my first Braxton Hicks Contraction. It was really weird, I was just walking along minding my own business, and then my tummy seized up. It didn't hurt, but I had to stop walking for a minute until it relaxed again. My midwife says these don't normally happen until later in pregnancy, but the Google machine tells me a different story, and made me feel normal. So I am sticking with Google for now.

Bubs is kicking and moving around a lot, still not strong enough to be felt on the outside by others, much to Husband's disappointment. Nevertheless, I really enjoy feeling it, which is surprising, because for as long as I can remember, I have just expected that I would hate it. That it would feel alien and weird, and awful. I was actually really nervous about feeling the kicks, but now that's all changed. I love it, I can sit for ages with my hand on the bump just waiting for the next one.

I am taking tomorrow off school, as I am absolutely exhausted. The discomfort of not being able to find a comfy position to sleep, the heartburn, the infrequent but painful round ligament pain, the swollen ankles and body that is already 7 kg heavier than it was five months ago, let alone the mood swing train, is taking its toll in a big way right now. At least I have my little kicker to keep me company! Maybe she'll be a soccer star!

May 24

Getting Resentful : A Pregnant Rant

It's true. Right now, there is very little that isn't making me very angry. Hateful even. Quite frankly, I have become an angry, bitchy, winging, tearful monster. I quote the Huggies website for week 21:

"Try to take some time every day, just to enjoy your pregnancy. This is a time when the early discomforts have (hopefully) settled, but the baby isn't so big it's causing you to be really uncomfortable. You could feel yourself in love with the world, a sense of wellbeing infusing every pore. Alternately, you could just be feeling fat and a little fed up. You may find you have a very short fuse when it comes to tolerating others and find yourself irritated by the smallest things. Make the time to exercise, which will help your body release endorphins, those feel good hormones."

Exercise

Well, it's clear which group I'm part of, and they suggest 'exercise' will help. That 'swimming is ideal'. Huh! Really? Have they tried fitting into a pair of togs lately? Or even figuring out the best way to shave your legs without—

a) Crushing the baby,

b) Falling over, or

c) Finding yourself unable to stand back up.

—in order to respectably don any type of swimming outfit? Not to mention the extreme self-consciousness that comes with looking like a baby whale. Hey, let's just make it more obvious, and jump into the pool! Find my distant relations and swim off into oblivion!

I want to exercise, I really do. But when it comes to the end of the day, I am far too exhausted to do anything. The other day, I even did what I swore as a beginning teacher I would never do. I put on a video for my class, because I was simply too tired to teach them anything.

Other People

Particularly men seem oblivious to the fact that comments you would never say to us when we aren't pregnant, are not suddenly ok to say just because we are.

I am a very short person. Therefore, apparently I look much more pregnant that I actually am. I am only just over half way there, therefore I anticipate that I am going to be pretty much rolling everywhere I go in the not too distant future.

I AM AWARE OF THIS! Calling me "chubby" is not ok. Saying, "It's ok that you're big, you're pregnant," does not make me feel better.

"You're only big in your belly," just makes me want to slap you. Telling me, "You look like you swallowed a basketball," is doing yourself no favours.

At least, I'm managing to avoid the tummy touching at the moment. Most of those who know me seem to have been forewarned.

Work

There is just way too much stuff to go into here.

I am on overload! I only officially work one part-time job. That is essentially 16 hours of work a week. Or so my pay cheque will tell you.

But, as any teacher will tell you, this is a lie. I do not work a mere 16 hours a week. No teacher does. I have 180 reports to write, 16 hours of lessons to plan a week, marking and photocopying to do for each class, not to mention the two hours of extra curricular choir rehearsals I run, a major musical performance evening coming up, as well as the half hour of lunchtime duty I am supposed to do each week. So, I get paid for 16, but essentially work at least 30 hours in my official part-time job.

Of course, let's not forget that I am also planning the giant interschool choir festival, which was my own monster that I created last year. People really loved it, and now it must continue. However, I have no funding, can't afford to pay anyone, and therefore am acting as director, secretary, media spokesperson, school liaison, presenter liaison, marketing and communications coordinators all by myself for free. This week, I put in 6-10 hours of work in my own time to get this thing up and running, recruit people to run workshops, and write and send out giant information packs to all the schools taking part. I have some help from others, but they are all also very busy.

And finally, this second baby monster I have created...

...my grand scheme to make a performance opportunity for

myself in order to not let this year's goals go to waste. The wonderful cabaret. It's fun, it's exciting, I think about it all the time. I have applied for rights, found the venue, found everyone who is involved, created the first script, and sorted out advertising. But now someone has pulled out...and it's suddenly become very stressful.

So—there you go. I bring it on myself. So what can I expect. But I am still mad.

Dads

Dads have it easy as far as I can see. They get a baby without any hard work really. They can take a week or two off work and then go back, knowing that they aren't needed because Mum is the feeding machine. They get time off to go and interact with adults on a daily basis. They get to continue all their favourite pastimes while Mum is pregnant. As far as I can see right now, their lives actually don't get disrupted all that much.

I know that I am probably completely wrong, but that's what I've been thinking this week, and it makes me MAD.

The Baby

Yet, with all of this going on, all I want to do is think about the baby. I just want to set up the nursery. I just want to stay home with it and not go back to work. I just want it to get here so that I can say, "Hi, little one." I just want someone to come and say, "It's all good, take a rest and feel baby move some more. Everything's under control and everything will be fine. I'll take it from here."

But in today's modern world, and with my own over ambitiousness, let's be honest. Who gets to do that?

May 28

No Going Back

Today, it hit me. I can't stop this. Literally, no matter what happens, I cannot get off this train. With only four weeks to go of the second trimester, and things getting a bit uncomfortable, suddenly everything is too close. Too soon. Too major. Too scary. Just....TOO!

Today, I narrowly avoided a panic attack in the staff room, as other mums laughed and jovially told me that there was no going back, and that's how it's going to be for the rest of my life. Cue loosen scarf, fan face, shake tingles out of hands. It's ok little hamster baby. We will do this together!

May 31

Midnight Panic

I am awake now. Completely awake. At least, that's what I'm telling myself. Baby is kicking up a storm, and has been for the past few hours now. I was finally drifting off to sleep, when I started to feel a bit uncomfortable. My heart was beating just a little too hard. My gut was feeling just a little too twisty. My shoulders were getting just a little too tense. I couldn't breathe right. I was too hot. I was about to Panic.

Normally, I try and make these blogs somewhat humorous, but right now, I just can't think how. I tried to calm myself down without getting out of bed. But it wasn't working, everything was getting worse. I was starting to feel on the verge of being very ill, that the next step was going to be huddled in the bathroom.

I don't know what it is. Or why it's happening again. Luckily I didn't fall asleep. Luckily I realised what was happening before it fully happened. But now what. I'm up. I'm tired. I'm scared to go back to bed, because it's all lingering in the back of my mind. My heart is still beating too hard. My stomach still doesn't feel right. Maybe I have food poisoning? I don't even know what I'm most worried about, what has brought this on? I can't go through with this pregnancy. I am so embarrassed about how I look. I can't remember anything. Everyone is looking at me all the time. Everyone thinks I'm too big. Everyone is judging everything I eat. I can't relax. I can't believe there is a living thing inside me. I can't make it stop. I have absolutely no control over it. I have no say anymore. I am trapped. I want this to be over. I want the baby to be here. I don't want to be pregnant anymore. I want a drink to calm me down. I want my body back. I want to be me again. What if I freak out too much and can't do it after all? Why did I even do this to begin with? I have too much on my plate. I have too much to think about. I want it all to stop. I don't feel any better yet. I'm scared this is going to keep getting worse. Maybe it won't even stop when baby gets here. I want to get off this ride now.

June 7

How Many People Does it Take to Fold Down a Stroller?

Today will forever go down in history, as the day of the stroller incident. We had some money saved. We needed a stroller. Put two and two together, today we shall buy a stroller! We had a fair idea of what we wanted and needed by now, nothing like those early days of buggy panic in Babycity. We wanted a three-wheeled one, that could go on outdoorsy walks, that could reverse the seat so we could see Baby, that reclined in multiple positions to fit baby as it grew, that had storage space and an adjustable handle—a must for tiny me—one that was in our budget (roughly $300) and most of all, one that was simple to use.

Seeing a major store was having another wonderful sale, we decided casually that we would check out their baby range. I had a baby brain moment and almost walked into a wall before getting on the wrong escalator, but we did manage to safely make it into the well-stocked baby department. So much to see! "Look at this!" "Oh this is cute!" "I hope someone will buy this for us!" "What is this for?" We were immediately sucked off track, looking at tiny clothes and hats and nappy bins, even a high chair appeared in the mix. It took a while for us to refocus on our ultimate goal. STROLLER! They had a good range, and we started pulling some out to play with. Some had awesome adjustable handles, but no reversing seat. Others had everything we wanted, but four wheels not three. Then we saw it.

The magical stroller of our dreams.

It literally had everything we needed. And at 40% off, we could even afford it! So we started to play with it. Within minutes we had figured out how to adjust the handles, recline the seat, remove the seat, reverse the seat, lock the wheels and attach the rain cover. All without having to look at the instructions. It was perfect!

That is, until we tried to collapse it.

For ten minutes we tried every button, pulley, lever, twisty nob, non-twisty nob, and slidey thing that we could find. Nothing worked. The stroller was still fully open. I buzzed a handily placed buzzer for assistance. She (hereafter Store Clerk #1 or SC1) came to our aid super speedily, but alas, was also unable to figure it out despite having even turned it upside down.

Without missing a beat, SC1 called the store manager. Because (as she eloquently put it), managers know everything. This proved inaccurate however, as 15 minutes later, neither the manager nor SC1 had succeeded in collapsing the stroller. I found this all highly amusing, as both Husband and I stood watching this now high-level drama unfold before our eyes. It was clear that they weren't going to give up until they had succeeded in collapsing this god damn stroller! ('scuse my language.)

Before long, we had four store clerks, a still-in-its-box buggy, and its accompanying instruction booklet, all working like crazy people to collapse it. But all to NO AVAIL!

That was about when they realised that the stroller and instruction manual they had gone to great effort to bring out of the back room was in fact, *not* for the stroller we were now desperately trying to dissemble. A similar model yes, but just different enough to have FOOLED US ALL! Cue: three store clerks, one manager, one now beat up display model, one opened and incorrect model buggy and now the correct model still in its box, complete with instructions on how to collapse.

The instructions, we then discovered, were in fact on the side of the stroller. But (thankfully) this still didn't help us. So none of us felt too bad. All up, it took an hour for all six of us to figure out how to collapse the child transporter. I couldn't stop giggling at the ridiculousness of it all. Even Hubby was grinning. He managed to set up and collapse the 'in the box' model multiple times with ease. I had a go, and also had little trouble. Everyone breathed a sigh of relief. I mentioned that it's a good thing we weren't mystery shoppers, but that they were pretty lucky that they had got a whole hours worth of paid training with real-life customers, and that I had now become so bonded with the stroller, I could hardly leave the store without buying it!

The store clerks were extremely relieved, all grinning, and no doubt keen for a lunch break after all that—perhaps even some wine, or something stronger. I was feeling like after all that, I should probably go buy them all lunch! So we bought the perfect stroller. But I am keeping the receipt!

And that, dear readers, is the answer to the question. It takes six people to put down a display model stroller. But only one to put down the model in the box.

June 19

Grumpy Cat

I've pretty much decided this week, that being pregnant, is the worst thing ever. Yes, I am aware that is a selfish, nasty, ungrateful thing to say. That there are plenty of people far worse off than me, so how can I be so naive and cruel! But I never said that I wasn't any of those things. I am very aware that society dictates that I should feel happy, glowing, lucky and like something miraculous is occurring within me. A new life is being created! I am a vessel producing a miracle! Everything is going OH SO WELL! Well, sorry world. That is not how I feel.

For three weeks now, all I have wanted, is to take a break from being pregnant. To step off this train for just a minute, and catch my breath. To lie on my stomach. To eat something without feeling like the devil. To be able to lift things without everyone around me crying, "NO!" To go for a run. To walk somewhere without being asked "When are you due?" To wear normal clothes. To get myself out of a chair without having to roll out. To stop having to tell people how I'm feeling. To walk without needing to pee constantly. Yes, everything is going normally. Yes, a lot of people would be so happy to be in my position. Yes, we had no trouble getting pregnant. Yay for us!

But to be honest, getting pregnant was fun. I feel like we were robbed of time spent 'trying'. It happened insanely fast. I thought we'd have ages to get prepared. I want to skip forward three months. I want the baby to be here. I am sick of feeling like I'm harbouring an alien. Watching my tummy move when I'm trying to relax is weird. Waking up to leg cramps is really not fun. I want control of my body again. I want to see the baby in its bassinet. To put it in its bouncer. To watch it sleeping. To take it for walks. To hold it. Sing to it. To finally get to know it. To go on family holidays with it. I am a horrible, horrible person. I can sense the backlash already. But this is my reality. And I'm not apologising for how I feel. Deal with it.

June 24

Ten Things to Never, Ever Say to a Pregnant Woman

There are many things that change when you are pregnant. Not just your body, your mindset, or your clothes. But also, apparently, the guidelines by which others are allowed to speak to you.

Below is a list of the ten weirdest, creepiest, and more than a little offensive and upsetting things that people feel OK saying to me since I got pregnant.

1. **Should you be eating that?** Now, this is offensive in two ways. Firstly, are you saying I'm fatter than I should be? Who gave you the right to judge anyway? And secondly, do you think I'm so heartless, that I don't think about what I'm eating almost constantly? Have you seen the list of foods to avoid when pregnant? Do you have any idea of the guilt trip placed upon pregnant women over eating almost everything from chicken, to Subway to salad that hasn't been washed?! Back off.

2. **Hi Chubby.** This was said in jest. He thought he was hilarious. I very nearly slapped him, but instead pointed out that I was unlikely to ever catch up to his stomach.

3. **How's the body holding up?** Said by another well-meaning man. But it's weird, and creepy. You don't, just don't ask a pregnant lady how the "body" is holding up. What kind of answer are you after? A truthful one with all the gory details, "Not great actually, my back hurts, my boobs hurt, I pee when I cough, when I sneeze and when I laugh, I am waking up with leg cramps, and everything is aching 100% of the time. Oh, did you want to know about the constipation and hemorrhoids too?" I didn't think so. So just don't ask.

4. **God, you're looking really pregnant today.** Thanks. I hadn't noticed. I certainly don't feel it.

5. **But since you're pregnant, you're obviously NOT on antidepressants.** I was so mad at this shop assistant that I fumed about this statement for the next two days. I wish that I'd said right there and then, "Well actually, I am." The judgment in that one statement was astonishing. I'm sorry, I am taking medications for my sanity while pregnant. Yet, here I am in your health store clearly taking an interest in keeping baby and myself healthy. What do you make of that? Am I evil in your eyes now? Do you think of me as some kind of callous mother who only thinks of herself? Do you think I didn't spend months weighing

up the pros and cons and researching EVERYTHING that could be found about taking this medication while pregnant? Well fuck you too, lady.

6. **You're allowed to look bigger, you're pregnant.** I know you're *trying* to make me feel better, but really, you're not. Now I just feel fat for a reason.

7. **The more you gain now, the harder it is to lose later!** Thanks for the heads up. I'll try to remember that when I've been thinking of nothing but cheeseburgers for 36 hours straight. Or when I'm so ravenously hungry I literally can't think straight. It's all about getting back in shape after all. Thanks for reminding me.

8. **No, you definitely CANNOT drink.** This debate has happened in front of me a number of times now. Mostly it happens when I mention how much I'd like a drink. I certainly never actually asked for one. I am in the 'don't risk it' camp at the moment, but I think that, like most things, the alcohol consumption in pregnancy thing is a personal choice. Forcing your opinion on me, particularly when you have a glass of merlot in your hand, have never been pregnant, or (god forbid) are a GUY, is tantamount to saying, "No,

you cannot have an abortion, it's bad, you are a bad person if you do that," and then going back to your child-free life.

9. **You should be excited.** I am excited. Are you kidding? I'm also in constant discomfort, have become some sort of magnet for people to stare at, am not sleeping, and feel ugly and disgusting. Sorry that my excitement isn't showing through for you at every possible moment, though I'll work on it.

10. **Surely you can't have THAT long to go, you're HUGE!** Just because I'm pregnant, doesn't mean telling me I'm huge is a compliment. Would you say that to someone who wasn't pregnant? Why do you think saying it to a pregnant woman is going to have any less of a negative effect? I go home each day feeling more and more self-conscious about how I am looking, precisely because of comments like this. Mostly they come from men. Bastards.

July 6

Ten Surprising Uses for Stomach Muscles

They say you never miss it till it's gone. So believe me, the use of my stomach muscles is now definitely gone! I challenge you to tie a three-kilo bag to your middle for a day, and then, try to do all these things:

1. **Vacuuming.** So much twisting, turning, reaching for plugs, pushing and pulling....

2. **Putting on Shoes.** When there is a bump this big in your way? Good luck!

3. **Shaving your legs.** See above. I'm not deliberately trying to return to my primitive roots, I promise.

4. **Carrying anything heavier than a plate**. Currently still possible....just. Tending to drag things behind me when possible.

5. **Reaching up high.** Things are increasingly being moved to lower shelves in our house. It looks like hobbits live here.

6. **Putting on pants/socks/stockings/underwear.** Ha. Ha. Ha.

7. **Tying shoe laces.** I gave up on this weeks ago. I only wear things that have zips or slip on easily now.

8. **Getting off (or out of) the couch/bed/bath/car.** I am stubbornly still refusing Hubby's generous and concerned offers for help with this. Stupid, stupid pride! Apparently I feel better acting (and sounding) like a stuck seal, than accepting help and getting up somewhat gracefully. I am not sure how much longer I can keep it up though.

9. **Rolling over in bed.** This now takes careful planning, kind of like a seven-point turn in a car, and I MUST be awake for it. Apparently.

10. **Laughing, coughing, sneezing**. Pain. Pain. Pain. Oh, and Poise of course. Thanks Poise.

July 08

29 Weeks - Depressed

Ok, I think it's fair to say that this is getting pretty difficult now. Physically, and mentally it is taking quite a toll. At the start, I was worried that I wouldn't be able to handle it because of all my anxiety and panic attack issues, but I've surprised myself on that front. For the most part, any anxiety I have had has been pregnancy related, and fairly normal concern about effects on the baby. I haven't been in a constant state of unrestrained panic or fear like I imagined I would be. I haven't been freaking out and feeling like there is an alien living inside me, that something abnormal is happening and I might die at any minute. I have made it through some pretty extreme panic situations without taking my normal miracle calming pills. I certainly haven't been wishing it would all go away constantly, and I definitely haven't gone crazy. Yet.

Perhaps that is all about to end, I don't know. All I do know, is that the last month has been hard. At first I wasn't sure if I was hormonal or actually getting legitimately depressed. I couldn't tell if I was just wanting to hide at home because I was actually tired, or if I was making excuses because I am becoming increasingly self-conscious about my changing appearance. I decided to wait it out. Figuring that things would get better. But they didn't. They got worse.

Last week I had a complete breakdown. I got teary, irritable, exhausted, couldn't sleep, couldn't be bothered getting up, getting dressed, or even eating properly. I desperately, desperately wanted it to be over. Baby must have had a growth spurt, because suddenly I can't put on my shoes, I can't bend, or reach for things, and even my Husband reckoned I'd grown in one afternoon. Literally, bigger since that morning, apparently.

I have been rude to friends, basically my inner monitor or think-before-texting/speaking seems to have vanished. I simply can't be bothered being tactful right now. I don't want to leave the house. I feel like everyone's eyes are constantly on me. I feel like the elephant in the room....which isn't far from the truth as far as I'm concerned. For someone who had pretty severe Social Anxiety right from eleven years old to my mid-twenties, these things are a big deal. I like to be invisible. I like to go about my day and not be noticed. I like to not be the topic of conversation. It is honestly, extremely disconcerting to suddenly find that I am public property.

Physically, things are tougher, walking is harder, and much slower than it should be. Sleeping with less than three pillows under my head makes the blood pound in my skull regardless of which way I am sleeping. Leg cramps can wake me, and I bite back a scream, and the pain lingers for days afterwards. Sometimes Baby kicks so hard, I actually worry that my skin can't possibly hold it in any longer.

I delayed getting pregnant for ages because I was terrified of the labour and morning sickness. Turns out, the things that are bothering me most, aren't even things I had considered. I never thought about actually BEING pregnant. I'd worried about physical things, but hadn't even contemplated the mental strain. Fair to say that I do have antenatal depression. Something I'd (stupidly) never even considered. I'd heard about postnatal depression, and been quite worried about that, but this? Washing and folding the baby clothes helps a bit. It lets me be a bit excited about what this hard work is leading up to. Perhaps I will start sleeping in the nursery to lift my mood. Oh, and we start antenatal classes tomorrow. That will hopefully be fun. In the meantime, I'm going to look up cat videos on YouTube.

July 22

Baby Showers

I had never been to a baby shower before last weekend, when I attended a friend's shower. It was sweet, and a nice group of friends all talking babies and making her feel super special. Plus, she looked amazing. Maybe that's why I'm suddenly feeling sad about my own shower, which is happening this weekend. There are a lot of people who can't make it, or who can't be there till later, plus my family all live in different cities and can't make it either.

I never had a hen's night, or a 21st party or really celebrated anything like that, so perhaps that's why this has taken on such importance in my head. I feel like it's a big deal, and I'm really excited about it. I have this weird notion that it's a really important thing, and that people should be making an effort to be there. That might explain why people not being able to be there or having to be late is really upsetting to me. Either that, or I'm just uber emotional this week. This is also true.

Baby has now grown to a point that I can feel 'bits' of it moving and sliding beneath my skin, rather than just general kicks and punches. It is very cool to feel what might be a foot or a hand or even a knee pressing against your hand as it rolls over or squirms. I still have five weeks until my maternity leave starts, but this baby has become the most important thing in my mind and my life, and I can't imagine how I'm going to make it through those five weeks. Not just because of how much of my brain space it occupies, but because I am increasingly immobile, uncomfortable and emotional. Let alone the distinct lack of anything work suitable to wear.

I hope that I am a good parent. I hope that I don't become someone who lives vicariously through my daughter. I hope that I can let her follow her own path and do what she enjoys doing. I hope that I can show her patience and understanding. I hope that I can give her the life she deserves.

July 24

The Morose Ghost

This, is a Morose Ghost:

This, is a morose Me

My husband says we are currently very similar, Morose Ghost and I.

Maybe that's because I no longer fit into my (once almost too big) favourite coat?

Or possibly my sudden inability to put on my own shoes and socks.

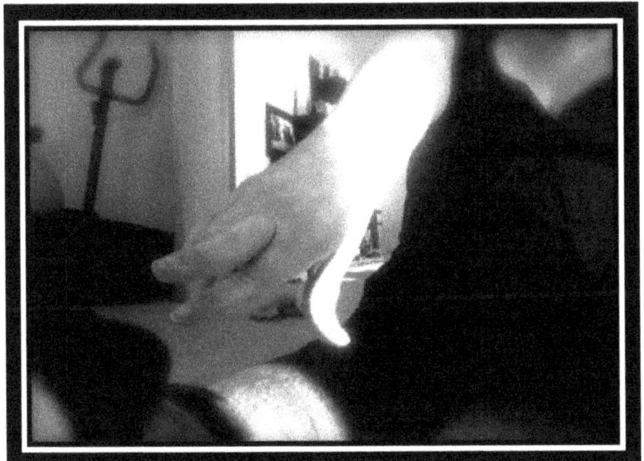

Or possibly the fact that I need this many pillows, arranged exactly like this in order to sleep even a little?

Or perhaps it's my cat's frequent looks of disdain?

Either way, it's time for...
MOROSE GHOST MOVER!
I'm off to look for them. I will let you know how I go!

July 25

Fighting the Morose Ghost: Steps 1 - 3

I have taken action. I've been transferred to a fantastic outpatient unit called mothers and babies, which specialises in mothers' mental health (funny that!). Tomorrow is the baby shower, and I'm super excited. I think it's because of the fact that three friends are organising it for me...and that is not something I've experienced before. Plus, my sister is flying down from shaky Wellington to be here and hang out before the baby arrives (SQUEEEE!) I talked to the midwife about maybe having to take maternity leave earlier, as getting around easily is becoming quite an issue. I will talk to the deputy principal about my options next week. But mostly, I have been focusing on getting my head straight again. Thinking positively, being excited, and trying to relax a little. Here are the top three tips from today:

1. Keep ignoring mother-in-law's well-meaning tips on keeping the house tidy with a new baby—or indeed at any time. Give Husband a 'talking to' when he passes such advice on. I may not run a tidy house, but dammit, I will run a happy house.

2. Run a bath. Do some Yoga. Read some more about Hypnobirthing. Do something to relax. This is something that is certainly keeping me super calm and relaxed about the next few months and the labour, so

I will be reviewing and talking about my experience with it as I go. So far....LOVING IT!

3. Ignore the dishes. Ignore the washing. Paint some drawers in the sunshine! They look FANTASTIC! I Will finish them tomorrow when my sister is here to help me move them...probably shouldn't have moved them by myself today, but hey! Couldn't resist. I hope you like them as much as I do Baby, 'cos they are all for you!

Verdict: Morose Ghost Mover is so far being effective. Win.

July 30

Feeling the Pressure

It's one thing to feel pressured to act and look excited all the time. It's another to have to keep pretending to feel great when you really don't, and people are constantly (and I mean constantly) asking you how you are, mentioning how you've, "got that walk down," giggling good naturedly at your struggles to do normal things and showering you with advice.

I no longer want to leave the house because of the inevitable questions, stories and knowing or curious looks that constantly bombard me from every angle. But there's been a new one cropping up in the last couple of weeks. "Are you going to have more than one?"

Excuse me?! I haven't even had this one yet! Before we got pregnant, Hubby and I had to frequently put up with the "When are you having kids?" question, particularly from my in-laws. It got to be so frustrating for me, that I eventually broke and said one day at dinner, "If you want grandkids, you're going to have to adopt them." I didn't mean it. But I really couldn't take it anymore. It's my relationship, we are just happy where we are, and it's actually none of your business when or if we do anything.

It seems as though regardless of at what point you're at in a relationship, people are always asking about the next stage. Will you ask him out? When are you moving in together? When are you getting engaged? Have you set a date yet?

How long do we have to wait for grandkids/nieces/nephews? Are you going to have more? Give me a break! My world has been utterly altered in ways I never could've imagined this year. And there is so much more to come. In no time at all, I will finally get to meet my baby. I'll finally get to hold her and look at her and protect her from all that pressure and judgment that we have been through. At least for a little while. So, are we having more kids? Let me have this one first.

July 30

Being Informed

AKA Society's Distinct Oversight In Leaving Women Unprepared For Pregnancy

I am not convinced that society has really moved on from the days when advertisements for morning sickness relief so that "she can cook breakfast again" were acceptable. It seems that pregnancy is still a huge secret, something you only get to learn about if you actually enter into its hallowed halls. How have we managed to get to a place, where we actively teach kids about puberty in schools, we give out our pre-adolescent girls 'sample packs' at age nine, we have baskets of condoms for the taking at many youth facilities, we see frequent and more graphic adds for tampons, liners and erectile dysfunction, and don't even mention the amount of sex and female nudity we see in the movies. Oh yeah—and the laughable fake pregnancies and birth scenes that we are treated to in TV and movies every now and then. Yet still, we are all allowed to enter adulthood and at some stage, our own pregnancy knowing very, very little about what 'being pregnant' actually entails.

Before I got pregnant, I knew precisely the following:

1. How to get pregnant.

2. That I'd get bigger and gain weight.

3. That morning sickness hit most women and was awful and could continue right through pregnancy

4. That labour hurt. A lot.

I may have had some vague notions surrounding things like stretch marks, practice contractions, that bleeding during pregnancy was bad and that pre-eclampsia was something I really didn't want. But in all honesty, that was it.

Before I got pregnant I was panicked about morning sickness, about the loss of control I'd have over my body and about the labour.

Before I got pregnant, I knew nothing. And nothing is what I expected.

Re. Ality. Check.

My body is giving me so many surprises lately, that I don't think I can take anymore. I now have to wake up and sit up, in order to roll over, as the weight of the baby makes my back click and my hips scream STOP. I am having to learn all the 'secrets of pregnancy' at a super fast rate. Because NOBODY tells you about it before you get there. I had never heard of colostrum or breast pads, or maternity pads, or breast pumps, or disposable hospital underwear before this year. I didn't know that you would start leaking colostrum before you'd even had the baby. I didn't know that your stomach stayed 'pregnant' after the baby was born. I didn't know that you'd bleed after giving birth, and most likely have to throw all your post-birth undies away. I didn't know about mucous plugs or the 'bloody show' or the sacrum, or that it really hurts in the first trimester to sneeze or cough, or that in the third trimester I'd get so huge I would actually need help getting in and out of the bed/bath/chair/car, be in constant pain and discomfort and want to sleep all the time.

Now that I am pregnant, I now understand why no one really talks about it.

It's horrible. It's gross. It's uncomfortable and it's incredibly personal.

But that doesn't excuse the lack of knowledge non-mothers have about pregnancy and birth. If you don't understand the reality, you aren't fully informed. If you are not fully informed, how can you possibly be expected to make the right decision about anything. It's the reason we are going through pregnancies freaking out at every new twinge or 'leakage' that occurs, because we really don't know what is or isn't normal. It's akin to going to the airport with a suitcase of your favourite beach clothes, getting on a plane with no idea where you're going, spending the whole time dreaming about oceans and sand, then landing in Alaska with no return ticket and being greeted by a guide speaking a language you barely understand who tells you, "Well, now you're here, this is how you survive."

Before I got pregnant, I was adamant that I'd have an epidural, gas, drugs, anything to get me through labour and out the other side, and more than likely was going to have an elective C-section in order to avoid it altogether.

Since I've been pregnant, I have completely changed my mind about labour, I now want it to be as natural as possible, because now I'm aware of what actually goes along with having a C-section, drugs or an epidural.

I can't wait to meet my daughter. But I want to meet her while I'm wide awake.

August 08

Baby Kick-Boxers, Bedtime Stories, Classes and Workouts

Baby is at 33 weeks now, and we are so close and yet still so far from meeting her. I read a blog yesterday about people getting told they were having a girl on four different occasions from four different scans, but the baby still came out a boy....so now Hubby and I are back to calling the baby "It" for a while.

Anyway, Baby is producing some epic kicks and rolls now. It's like having a tiny acrobat in my tummy, yet I never seem able to get Hubby to see or feel the really big moves. It's like a cruel trick, I alert him to what's happening, he eagerly looks or feels, and Baby stops. Just long enough for him to decide Baby doesn't like him, and for him to go away feeling glum. On the upside, we (I mean Husband) is reading *The Faraway Tree* aloud each night for Baby to get used to his voice and (hopefully) to boost its love of stories and general awesomeness. If nothing else, I'm rather enjoying being transported back to my own childhood each evening, although the stories seem rather a lot more scary than I remember, and I'm wondering if they aren't a source of my original anxiety issues—strong winds meaning bad things, getting trapped in strange places with no way out.

But enough of that! I've decided that the third trimester is designed to force mothers to strengthen their arms in preparation of the impending baby carrying duties. I sure feel like I am working out my biceps on a regular basis, pushing myself up out of bed, off couches, pulling myself out of the car, lifting myself out of the bath. Not just that, but the number of times I must wake up each night is certainly good training for living with a newborn....otherwise what's the point?

I think I have everything ready now. My (expensive!) very awesome nappy bag arrived last week, and I already have it packed and ready to go with whatever Baby might need. I really just want It to arrive, so that I can see and hold and cuddle and just....be with It. I am really struggling to keep my head in the game at work, and not just because walking while carrying laptops and books and folders is now a super undesirable activity, but because the date of arrival is drawing ever closer and I just get too excited to worry about whether 'Johnny' understands what a city state is, or if 'Jane' really gets what I mean when I say, "Four beats per bar," while she nods in agreement. But I'm doing my best, I try to get up and walk around the classroom as much as possible. I try to still think of and create interesting activities if I can. Next week I am organising a giant choir festival, which I unwittingly created last year, so once that is over, the countdown can really begin.

Hubby and I have all but abandoned out antenatal classes in favour of the hypnobirthing ones. Antenatal classes seem to focus on every possible bad outcome, all the pain relief available, and all of the medical interventions. And to be honest, they freaked me out. After hearing about the three stages of labour over the course of three weeks, my anxiety had skyrocketed again and I was starting to have panic attacks when I was left alone for any amount of time. On the other hand, hypnobirthing focuses on the fact that birth is a normal process, it's happened for thousands of years, all over the world, to mothers in far less favourable conditions than ours. It teaches you that your body and the Baby know what to do, and that in order for that to happen best, the mother needs to be as relaxed as possible. We have another session tomorrow, and needless to say, if nothing else, it is definitely keeping me calm, positive and relaxed in the lead up to the delivery day.

In the meantime, we are going to see the movie *The Conjuring* tonight....and YES, I did check with my midwife that it was ok.

Look! Baby is rolling over now!! ......oh wait, you missed it.

August 16

Insanity at 34 Weeks

There used to be a drug called Miltown. It claimed that, "Pregnancy can be made a happier experience," by the drug's ability to reduce stress, anxiety and insomnia associated with being pregnant. I'd like to know what side effects you caused that meant you are no longer curing 88% of pregnant women of anxiety, insomnia and emotional upsets. Where were you last weekend when I had a complete meltdown and for some reason thought that locking my poor darling Husband in the garage was the appropriate response to what had begun as a minor argument.

NB - my sister talked me into letting him out within 10 minutes via text. He had by that time, got a sleeping bag and made a bed in the back of the car. We'd both like to thank my sister for quickly texting some sense into me. I realise that I can now expect that to be used against me for pretty much anything that pops up in the future. There is nothing ok about what I did.

I was temporarily insane. For an entire weekend.

That said, it is fair to say that things are heating up. At 34 weeks, I am now having night sweats. Which, let me tell you, are a little more intense than the average 'I'm-too-hot-must-remove-some-covers' night sweats. These involve me waking up LITERALLY DRENCHED, having to change pyjamas, wipe off with a flannel and let the bed air out. By which time, I am wide awake and once again need to pee. When I get back the sheets are freezing and still damp, so I've recently taken to sleeping on a towel, but that only stops the bottom sheet getting wet. Somehow, my Husband manages to sleep through all of this. I did wake him up once, to check that I wasn't imagining it, but it took him so long to awaken from his peaceful slumber, that there wasn't much left to see. The midwife says it's hormonal, and there are no tricks that she can recommend to help. But I already knew that, because by the time I asked her about it, I'd already researched it on Google. Little Baby is now taking up so much room, I am worried about how much space can be left to occupy. She is kicking and rolling and punching up a storm, and has an uncanny knack of ensuring my bladder gets pommelled at least three times a class, twice when I'm driving, and anytime I'm sitting somewhere very difficult to get up from. Which is giving those pelvic floor muscles little emergency incontinence 'drills'. "Are you ready? No? Well I don't care! WHACK!"

I'm managing my anxiety relatively ok, the hypnobirthing and relaxation is most definitely helping. All the same, I am finding that if I am left alone for too long, I start thinking far too much, and start to panic a little....ok a lot, about labour and my ability to cope with sleep deprivation, to be a good mum, to be a good wife, to be able to let go of a lot of things and make friends with other mums. We are the first of our friends to have a baby, so it's a little daunting.

On the other hand, I've got all these plans for when Baby gets here. We are going to make an awesome potted vege garden....or rather, I will, and Baby will be there in her bouncinet, carefully covered in the baby safe sunscreen that I bought this week. We will go for walks with her in the pram, and we will visit library story times, and play groups, and we will go to mums 'n' bubs sessions at the movies when she's old enough and..and...and.....there is just SO MUCH FUN WE WILL HAVE!

Please don't be late Baby! I have nowhere left to grow, and I can't wait to hang out with you!

August 21

On Men I Want to Punch in the Face—and Some Other Stuff

So here I am again, for the second time this week, at home rather than at work, and feeling completely EXHAUSTED. My hormones have reached yet another level of crazy, although this week they seem to be aimed out our government instead of my Husband, which is a relief. Still, my feelings of utter rage towards the PM's snarky-smug-rich-pasty-ruining-my-dreams-of-home-ownership-face on the news do leave us both concerned about the safety of our television.

I'm having some intense dreams, mostly about the state of the planet and the guilt I feel about bringing a new person into it, in its current state of affairs. I even dreamt there was a public service announcement on the news saying that this generation of kids would be the last the earth would see because things had gotten so bad! Needless to say—GUILT TRIP! I am now looking into nappy recycling and installing a rainwater tank and perhaps finding a way to collect our wastewater for the garden and learning how to compost properly. Trying to plan my vege garden to be as effective as possible in the space we have, and even, perhaps, just being ready to go be survivalists in the bush.

Husband's not so keen on that one. Plus, as renters (he calmly points out), "Probably installing a wastewater collection system is not such a great idea." Husband says, "We can do that when we own a house."

"Own a house?!" is my incredulous reply. "At this rate the # $ &* #??!!!! PM's snarky-smug face isn't going to let us own anything!!!!"

It is a little infuriating, that two nearly 30 year olds with a total of 13 years of University education between them, who have impeccable credit ratings, have never failed a bond inspection or been in trouble with the law, who have both worked full time up till now with no kids, cannot foresee owning a house in the next five years, probably more.

A lot of homeowners try to make me feel better by saying things like, "but you don't have to pay rates," and "You aren't responsible for the upkeep of your house." True, but we also get inspected every three months, we can't own a dog, we can't paint or decorate, we can't put in the dream vege garden from my head, we are constantly planning to have to move, and ironically we are paying more in rent than we would be if we had a mortgage. I'm worried that our baby will draw on the walls. I am worried that something will break and it will be our fault. The amount of stress involved in a flat inspection is definitely not ok. So yes, I still dream of owning my own house, despite our current house being a super awesome place to live.

Anyway, back to Baby.

I am flitting between calm belief that I can do this without problems, and then overwhelming anxiety that:

a) I will force us into an emergency birth by panicking and letting too much adrenalin and cortisol into my system. Or,

b) I will be a terrible mum. Or,

c) I have already ruined my baby's life by eating too much McDonalds whilst pregnant.

I have washed most of the baby stuff now, such cute clothes that I hope she fits. My new fear is that she will be 8 pounds or more and not fit any of the cute newborn stuff we have for her! The staff at school are running a sweepstake on the weight, which is kind of more than a little embarrassing. Much as I love my job, and know that I will probably go crazy when maternity leave starts, it's a bit of a relief to not have to be there sometimes. To have a break from feeling like a new breed of hippo while I lug my laptop between classrooms, or go all the way to the photocopy room only to realise I've forgotten to bring the photocopying with me. On Monday I found myself in the deputy principal's office desperately trying not to become 'the crying pregnant woman', as I explained that I didn't think I'd be able to last until the end of next week, as the pain associated with walking (feet, back, hips, groin, sides, legs...pretty much everything), and the exhaustion of not sleeping longer than an hour at a time (night sweats, toilet, rolling over, nightmares), all combined with my overwhelming self guilt trip over my declining teaching standards as a result (lack of energy, lack of excitement, sitting down all the time) were all making things pretty near unbearable. He was super understanding and told me that I can take time off whenever needed, and that everyone is in place to take over my classes from Monday. Of course, I didn't mention about the douchebag male staff members making teasing comments (about my walk, my weight, my mood, the labour, the birth, my teaching) that make me want to cry. Of course, they think they are absolutely hilarious.

They are lucky I don't have the balls to actually punch them in the face.

September 4

Leaving Work - Four Weeks Till Due

I am now officially 36 weeks and three days pregnant. Which according to midwives and doctors (but not hypnobirthers) means that in four days, Baby will be 'full term'. Which means that she will no longer be considered premature if born now. That seems crazy.

What's crazier is that there is an actual being that looks like a newborn baby kicking up a storm in my belly. It's hard to imagine at times, as the shapes created by, and the intensity of the kicking/punching/rolling, are oftentimes a little terrifying. I have been woken up by them a couple of times, it feels like she's trying to kick her way out of my stomach and burrow into the mattress. I have been assured that this is probably not the case.

My maternity leave started this week. The weekend and last day of work was a bit of a mind trip. I love my work. I can't imagine not working. I have had my own income since I was 11. I have always worked and since leaving home have never been dependent on anyone. I feel that it wouldn't be so bad if I knew when I was going back. But the nature of my contract is that I won't be going back. My position won't be filled by someone on a fixed term maternity leave contract whereby I can come back to it without any issue in a year. If I want to go back, I will have to hope there is an opening and apply for it along with everyone else.

Being part of a generation where women are expected to work, to have a career, to study, to be smart and to earn money, in an economy where one income is rarely enough to support a family, the new life just around the corner for me is a very scary and somewhat counterintuitive prospect. I'm supposed to give up everything I've studied and worked for, give up my income, halt my career path for an unspecified period of time, to stay home, look after a baby, keep the house, rely on my husband's income and.......and what?

There have been moments I have wondered if it wouldn't be a lot easier if gender roles were a lot more specific. If we (girls) weren't expected to be everything, and do everything to be 'equal'. If we could be considered successful and smart regardless of whether we were stay-at-home mums or career girls. I remember my Mum saying frequently that stay-at-home mums work harder than anyone else and she wished they could get paid. Before she had us kids, she was a career girl and good at it. I think that the change to being a Mum was probably a shock for her too. But she never really said it. She didn't get a job again until I was well into my teens. But then she stopped as quickly as she started. I think Dad didn't like the thought that he wasn't earning enough. Dad brought in the money, Mum looked after the house. I never questioned it.

I think of the early childhood memories I want to create for my daughter. How I don't want to put her in daycare right away. How I don't want to have more children right away, because I want her to be the kid in the family for a decent amount of time, not the helper. That I want her to feel safe and loved by her family. How I desperately want to do right by her and how the closer she gets to arriving, the more I'm suddenly willing to sacrifice to make sure that she has the best possible life I can give her.

Then I remember how much I love my job, and I am at square one on the cognitive dissonance board once again. It's only been three days on maternity leave, and I already have lost track of what day it is. I seem to be texting my midwife at least twice a day with questions I could probably Google answers for, but I would rather not freak myself out at this late stage.

"Baby isn't moving as crazily as normal, should I be worried?"

"Maybe. If you are worried, you could come in for a scan, but then you'll be on the doctor's radar, and if they get overly cautious they could try to induce you. See how it goes tonight."

"Is this increase in *insert bodily fluid here* normal, or am I going into labour?"

"Is there blood? No? Then you are not in labour."

"I've got really painful period-type cramps..."

"See above message."

"My Husband has gastro, if I catch it will it hurt the baby?"

"No, Baby will be fine. You'll be pretty miserable though."

Going to find the Dettol now. Husband is sleeping in spare room. Hand sanitiser everywhere! Yes, poor dear Husband has gotten sick. Which sucks for both of us. He feels rubbish, I feel rubbish for not feeling more enthusiastic about looking after him.

NB - my midwife is actually really cool. Not like the above semi-fictional replies might indicate.

Nesting has taken control of my psyche in a way I never anticipated! Remember those drawers I started to paint? Well they are finally finished and look amazing! With red, green, blue and yellow drawers with different coloured drawer knobs.

AMAZING!

Of course, after this success, my redecorating instincts could see no limits, and I proceeded to spend an afternoon recovering our boring dining chairs. More time was spent establishing a hanging vege garden on the patio. Making four batches of muffins for the freezer. Making prepared slow cooker meals for the freezer. Washing all the baby clothes. Doing an epic clothing 'purge', and generally just trying to get rid of as much crap as possible from all random areas of the house.

By Monday I was tired, so I stopped. Then Husband got sick. Then it rained and hailed a bit. Now I don't know what day it is anymore! It probably isn't helpful that I haven't changed the calendars yet, but I'm too scared to do so. Because then it really WILL be September and Baby is nearly here. I'm not mentally ready for this yet!

September 16

Coming, Ready or Not

Last weekend, just three hours before my pregnancy app alerted me to the fact that I had made it to 37 weeks, my waters broke. Little Bean was born 25 hours later at 4.44 am after a prolonged labour which didn't go to any of my plans. I couldn't have a water birth because my own waters broke too early and the doctors were worried about infection. Baby was in a posterior position, which meant a drawn out early labour, and a strong urge to push at just 5 cm dilated, as well as more painful contractions early on. Rest assured, I quickly found a new love of epidurals, and Little Bean entered the world with the help of forceps, managing to avoid a C-section by one contraction. It was the single most painful and overwhelming experience of my life so far.

Baby was taken to NICU just a few hours after being born, which was super hard. Nothing really prepares you for the sight of your baby in an incubator, connected to tubes, drips and a breathing apparatus. My heart broke, and that was the first meltdown. She was in there for two days, having antibiotics to help sort her breathing out. Once she was finally out, I was told we could go home the next day, and this was after night three where I had a second complete meltdown at eleven at night, basically begging the midwives to let me go home right then and there. They tried valiantly to convince me that leaving right then was not a good idea. It was too dark, it wouldn't be good for the baby, and my Husband was at home asleep. But nothing would help me. I was sharing a room, which I hate, the curtained off section I was in had no sunlight or view of any kind, the other lady's baby wouldn't settle, so regardless of how well Little Bean was sleeping, I was not. The midwives told me that there was no reason we couldn't go home tomorrow. Baby was doing much better, all her bloods looked good, and the talk was that I would be discharged in the morning. With this stuck firmly in my mind, I nodded in acquiescence to have them take Baby away for a few hours so I could attempt to sleep (not that she was the one keeping me up).

At five in the morning, I was woken gently by another midwife, "Jess," she asked, "Did Baby have a bump behind her ear earlier? Where the forcep mark is?" I felt my anxiety rising instantly as I shook my head, "No, it wasn't swollen, it was fine."

"Ok," She sat down next to me. " It looks like the forcep graze may have become infected and the doctors want to put her on a three-day course of antibiotics." She was watching me very intently. I felt like I was being sucked into a black hole. "So I can't go home?" She shook her head. "No, she will need to be monitored here." I was silent, but my breathing was erratic as I tried to fight back the next onslaught of tears and anxiety.

"What can we do to make it easier for you to be here?" she asked quietly. I shook my head, I couldn't think beyond having to stay here, I couldn't see anything that would make it better.

"What if we were to find you your own room?" I looked at her, "Is that possible?" It seemed impossible.

"We've been talking about it, and we are going to see what we can make happen."

This past week has been a blur of nights becoming days becoming nights again. I did get my own room in the hospital finally, and as soon as I did, my panic attacks diminished, my milk started to come in, and my overwhelming need to keep some form of control in a 2x3 meter space disappeared.

We are finally home now. It is making a huge difference. Slowly things are starting to become a bit of a routine. Sleep, change baby, feed baby, put baby back to bed, try to get food for yourself, try to sleep again, repeat ever three hours. The lack of sleep, and getting breastfeeding going is an endless, ongoing exercise in endurance. Let's see what next week brings, although I don't know when that will be. I have no idea what day it is anymore. I'm not sure why I care about that. As though it somehow makes a difference. In the meantime, Baby and I will continue to get to know each other. I love it when she makes eye contact and holds your gaze. I love that she settles on me so easily and that I can calm her when others cannot. I've always been slightly afraid of babies, and now suddenly here is one that actually calms down on me, rather than crying even louder.

September 27

Sleeping Like A Baby…

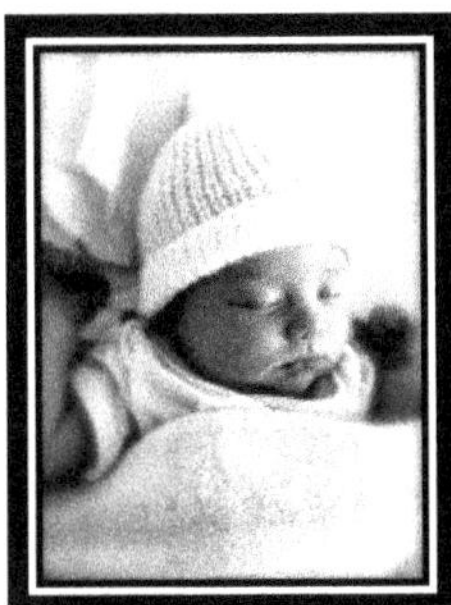

…is a very inaccurate metaphor. Babies do not sleep soundly. Nor do they sleep quietly. Nor do they sleep for long periods at a time. In fact, newborns are really, freaking noisy sleepers. They sound like asthmatic hedgehogs dreaming of running, or snuffling, or possibly eating and drowning. Yes, at the same time. Not only do they not sleep quietly, but they don't sleep for llong. Maybe four hours in a stretch if you are lucky, and naughtily disobeying your midwife's strict instructions to feed them every three hours. Looking after a baby is best summed up in one word.

Relentless.

For the first week of this one's life we were locked in a hospital where kind midwives would take her away in the middle of the night if my thoughts of, "Please can we give her back now," were becoming too obvious on my face. I didn't know who she was. I felt cheated out of that magical moment where your heart breaks when you first lay eyes on your baby. I kept waiting for it to happen.

For the second week, we were at home. Hubby and I putting in a valiant 'one night on, one night off' team effort. Ourselves, subsisting on meals made by friends, eaten in shifts while the other comforted/fed/changed her. Stoically taking it in turns to have meltdowns and question through exhausted tears our wisdom in taking this step, and our ability to actually keep *ourselves* alive, let alone one so helplessly dependent

This week was week three. My motto has become "Keep it together" played on repeat across the hours, which are now measured in feeds and sleeps and nappy changes. Hubby is now back at work, and we three have survived the first real week of the rest of our lives. Our initial chance to bond with our daughter may have been interrupted by hospital incubators, IV lines and feeding tubes, but each day at home, I am getting to know her a little more. Each day I give her a few more kisses. Each day she feels a little bit more like she's my own, and a little less like a stranger. Each day we are keeping it together a little stronger, and becoming more of a family. Post-natal depression hasn't got the best of me yet, and I intend to keep it that way.

October 16

Making Yogurt at 2am

How did I come to be making yogurt at 2 am? I wonder this myself, as I stand in the light of the fridge shaking the bottle waiting for the kettle to boil. In the lounge, Baby is wide awake in her bassinet, apparently unaware that 2 am is not an ideal time for such wakefulness. But she is content to be so, she is fed, changed, swaddled, quiet. Just incredibly awake.

In the past five and half weeks, I have learnt that I invariably will choose to sleep rather than eat, unless I force myself to do otherwise. I have discovered that I can eat dinner using just my non-dominant hand, although steak proves a challenge. I have also found that it is by far easier to simply remain awake, than it is to allow yourself to start falling asleep and be woken ten minutes later when you are actually starting to drift off.

"Sleep when the baby sleeps" is great advice. However, you never can be sure when Baby is actually going to stay asleep,

or for how long, or if you should take this opportunity to eat or shower rather than sleep as it might be six hours before the next chance you get to do so and in the meantime you remain covered in milk. I have also learnt that *The Ellen Show* is on four times a day, so if I miss the first screening, I have three more chances to watch it. Today I managed on the fourth try. Just. (It's the small things).

I am thinking about all of this, in a weird fuzzy slideshow of images as the fridge starts to beep as if saying, "I've been open too long." I realise the kettle has boiled. Baby is making contented snuffling noises in the lounge, the heat pump is making a racket, pretty sure it's broken, what am I doing standing here?

Close the fridge. After four nights of roughly two to four hours of sleep and 3.30 am starts, I had finally had a meltdown. Phoning my Husband at work, begging him to please come home early so I could go to bed. Baby wouldn't settle. Nothing that worked yesterday was working today. After last week's high of 'I can do this motherhood thing', I had crashed into the depths of 'I need to get away from this' territory.

Nothing was going well, feeding had become a nightmare after waking up with the third bout of mastitis I'd had in two weeks. I could write an entire blog post about the issues I'm having with feeding, but that's another story. At least she's cute. Lucky for me, I'm not a single mum, and my wonderful Husband did manage to come home early. I was in bed by 4 pm, asleep soon after. My boobs woke me up at 7, at which point I was forced to get up for their sake. Take Baby off Husband so that he can make dinner, "She's not slept yet," he tells me. I believe him. Back in bed by 8 pm, Baby finally asleep, I'm asleep an hour later. Miraculously slept till 1 am (bob alarm on overdrive by then). Send tired Husband to bed. "Baby slept till midnight," he tells me. I'm impressed. A four-hour stretch. I decide to sleep in the lounge so he can get unbroken sleep. That's how I came to be here. Standing in the light of the fridge, making yogurt at two in the morning. Having got enough sleep to feel vaguely functioning again, I finally achieve the task I've been meaning to do for six weeks now—make yogurt. Win.

October 23

Sharenting and Conspiracy Theories

Sharenting:

Combination of two words: parenting and sharing. When parents share too much of their children's information, pictures and private moments online, mostly on Facebook.

1. That Mom is way overboard with her sharenting on Facebook.

2. Everyone is going to know everything about that poor kid because his/her parents aren't careful with their sharenting.

Reference:
http://www.urbandictionary.com/define.php?term=Sharentin
g

In the days before Baby (hereafter known as BB), I swore I'd never be one of those parents who sharent. I was adamant I didn't want my baby plastered all over the Internet until she was old enough to decide if she even wanted her photo there in the first place. BB, I was often amused and equally bemused by the photos and updates others would post about their kids. Regularly thinking, "Why?" and telling myself with much confidence, that I would not put my Facebook friends through the same daily wall-trailing ordeal. BB, I was never going to be that person. Yet here I am. Being that person. Because finally, I get it. I simply can't help myself.

Facebook is a place to spread news about your life, your highs and lows, achievements and failures, and at the moment, they are ALL directly related to Baby. Everything I do, think, feel or dream about is about her. Little Bean is my life. BB, weekends meant time off, sleep-ins and movie nights. Now they are two days where I have help. Where I can potentially achieve something that I've been trying to do all week. BB, I thought about career paths, performing, lesson planning and students. BB, I sang daily. Now my thoughts are about when I will next grab some sleep. How I will eat my next meal. If I have time to have a shower, or should I take her in with me. Why is she crying? Is she too hot, too cold, hungry, tired, windy? Does she want a pacifier? What time did she last eat? Is she about to sleep properly? How long has she slept for? Baby. Baby. BABY. BABY!

BB, I wondered frequently why no one ever talked about labour, pregnancy, having babies. I wondered why I was a 27-year-old female who knew next to nothing about what to expect. Wondering how I managed to get to this stage in my life and still be so ignorant. Now I know.

The survival of the human race depends on our knowing NOTHING IN ADVANCE.

It's the world's biggest conspiracy. A secret kept for thousands of years by everyone who has ever had a child, in an effort to keep others from knowing the truth. In a selfish attempt to bring more people into the fold to commiserate with and wonder, "WHAT HAVE WE DONE?", "I WANT MY LIFE BACK", "WE'VE MADE A TERRIBLE MISTAKE!" Because pregnancy is a breeze compared to the first three weeks after birth. Those weeks are a blur of tears, pain, extreme sleep deprivation and horrible fears that you aren't meant to be a parent after all. Those weeks make you wonder, "What have we done?"

But then, Baby smiles.

Little Bean has started smiling. Not often yet, but she has. I finally felt the Heart Glow that everyone talks about. I realised what it's all about. That's why no one talks about it. Because if people knew how hard it is, and how the one thing that makes it all worth it is a simple smile, they wouldn't have kids. They wouldn't go through all that hell. They wouldn't feel the heart glow. Because they wouldn't be able to comprehend, how something so small can make all that hell worth it.

November 2

The Parent App

If you need help to give your life an overhaul, The Parent App is the greatest App you will ever download. It will give you fulfillment, challenge you, puzzle you, and provide you with endless hours of entertainment and joy on a scale no one can describe and which no other app can provide. If you want to change your life, and you've been looking for an easy way to do it quickly, this is the App you've been looking for! Finding Candy Crush too easy? This app can guarantee to keep you constantly on your toes! The goal is simple. Stop the baby from crying. Keep the baby from dying. There are no other rules. Simpler to play than Plants vs Zombies, and rewards you with more than just sunshine!

Reviews:

Kelly780

***** Best Feeling Ever

"This app is amazing, getting it is the best thing I ever did. Waking up to it is the best feeling ever!"

JohnJay9

*** Some Bugs

"There are some fairly minor bugs to sort out, but overall, this App really changed my life for the better."

Iceberg20567

* Don't do it.

"This app destroyed my life."

Please take the time to read the terms and conditions before committing to purchase.

Terms and Conditions

By committing to purchase you are stating that you have read these terms and conditions.

The Parent App requires access to your entire life. Your calendar, your family, your friends, your job, your social life, your house, your ability to leave your house, your ability to travel, your ability to sleep, your ability to watch a movie uninterrupted, your ability to eat a meal with both hands, your ability to rinse the conditioner out of your hair, your ability to bathe, your desire to have sex, your mental stability and your notion of personal space and your ability to spend time alone.

Warning

This game has two goals that need to be met constantly in order to keep it from destroying your entire existence. There are many right ways to achieve these goals, however only one will apply at any given time. The correct solutions are programmed to change at random, and without warning. This app will run constantly, and once installed will take priority over every other app you are attempting to run at any given time. It cannot be deleted or uninstalled. It cannot be exchanged or returned for a refund. It will run 24 hours a day, 7 days a week from the moment you activate it, and is set to demand your attention frequently, at random, and mostly at your inconvenience. By clicking "I Accept", you are stating that you have read, understood and agree to all the above. We accept no responsibility for any harm or mental distress brought about by this app.

Good thing no one ever reads the T & C's!

November 9

This Too, Shall Pass

Two days after Baby was born, I suddenly realised that I had made a really big mistake. I wasn't meant to be a mother. I wasn't cut out for dealing with a newborn. I didn't feel that overwhelming rush of love that everyone talks about, instead, when I looked at her, all I felt was fear. Fear that my life was over. Fear that I wasn't up to the task. Fear that I had let her down already, that I would be a disappointment to her, that I would never feel the love that I was supposed to feel—had EXPECTED to feel—for this tiny, brand new human.

Tomorrow, she will be nine weeks old, and last week, I took a rare moment of quiet, to read through this entire blog from the start. I realised how far I have come, how far *we* have come, and how much I have changed. Before Little Bean was born, I was bored. A lot. I was anxious about things that I had far too much time to think about, and I generally spent my days pondering the future, or ruminating on the past. I have not been bored even once, since she was born. I've been frustrated, tired, overwhelmed, scared and elated, but I have not been bored. I am far less anxious now about life than I can remember being in a long time, perhaps this is because I haven't got the time to over-think, to plan out the worst possible scenario or let anticipation take over. Or perhaps it's because suddenly, I realise how precious each moment is. Each sleepless night is the only one I get with her. Every tired morning and exhausted afternoon are only fleeting moments in her life, and nothing lasts. I am spending far less time dreaming of, or worrying about the future, rather, I am suddenly realising how precious each moment with her is.

Everyone keeps saying, "It's only temporary", "This too shall pass", and "It's just a phase." Sayings (I assume) meant to help parents envisage a light at the end of a tunnel when everything becomes too overwhelming. But they also serve as stark reminders that everything is only temporary, that this will pass, and that once it's gone, it won't come back. How far I've come since the start of this year. How much I have learned. I am most definitely a different person now. My daughter has changed me in ways I never dreamed. I am more patient, far calmer, and somehow more in control of how I react to situations. That's not to say that on the inside I am not freaking out and completely losing it, but outwardly, I am able to maintain my composure, at least for a while. I have a friend who is in their third trimester, and I suddenly find myself a source of advice, an experienced 'parent', who apparently looks like they've 'got this parenting thing down', to outsiders. I certainly don't feel that way! It seems ridiculous that I'm offering advice at all!

November 17

Growing Up Catholic

One of the, dare I say, many unfortunate by-products of growing up Catholic, is that you feel guilty about everything. You feel a constant need to confess. All the time. It NEVER GOES AWAY!

When you become a parent, you also feel guilty. All of the time.

It DOES NOT STOP!

So when you combine the two, you end up with a guilt overload. It's like crashing two atoms together and creating your own guilt universe. Everything you don't do perfectly becomes a catastrophe, everything you think and want for yourself is a terribly selfish thing, and you feel like you should simply go to your room and hide, or beg for forgiveness, or cry, or say sorry, or do all of those at the same time!

Today is one of those days where I would give almost anything for someone to take my daughter for the day, simply so I can sleep for longer than two hours at a stretch and regain a sense of sanity. But even the fact that I am thinking that, makes me feel like a horrible mother. No, a horrible PERSON, akin to Stalin, or Sauron, or Darth Vader.

Thinking these thoughts makes me feel...

...Guilty.

The days where I wished this disappeared for a while, but now they have returned with a vengeance. I'm really not sure why. Perhaps it's because my shoulders and back are aching from looking down at and holding a feeding baby for hours a day. Maybe it's because I'm so run down, I feel like I have been on the brink of having the flu for two weeks now and am waking up in-between night feeds with headaches and a runny nose. Or perhaps it's to do with the increasing episodes of Mummy guilt over things I'm doing wrong, and encroaching anxiety as I realise how I truly could not cope if something unspeakable did happen.

At ten weeks, these are some valuable lessons I have learnt.

1. Cutting baby fingernails is a next to impossible and extremely dangerous endeavor. Best to mitten up their little hands or bite the nails while they are feeding. But even that can lead to disaster and screaming and GUILT.

2. The old wives tale (and popular opinion on 'The Natural Parent' Facebook page and numerous mummy forums online) that breast milk will cure sticky eye (and all manner of other ailments) is a lie. In fact, it can make them much, much worse and you will end up feeling extreme GUILT when you do go to the doctor and they ask if that is what you have done.

3. Going to the doctor is free for under 5's, even after hours. I feel GUILTY that I waited till Sunday to take her, when I should have taken her on Friday. I should have been more proactive.

4. Don't pick a baby up with one hand. No matter how much you desperately want to finish your chocolate bar. This can lead to falling babies, babies knocking heads on things, screaming babies and extreme GUILT for you.

5. Babies don't always let you know when they need a new nappy. You have to remember to check and change them. If you don't remember and suddenly it's been six hours and when you do check they are really in need of a new one, guess what, you will feel very GUILTY!

6. Always have a cloth over your shoulder. Ironically, I don't have one there right now. Failing to do this won't make you feel guilty. It will just create more washing.

7. Babies need to be entertained. They need 'stimulation'. They need it from you. If you are however, only getting about five hours maximum of broken sleep each night, then you will feel GUILTY for not being enthusiastic about this, and instead wishing that your baby would just go to sleep.

So, here I am, feeling like I am a horrendously lazy mother. Clearly I don't care or love my child enough because all I want to do is sleep. I don't want to spend the next hour repeating silly baby noises and poking her nose and forcing myself to smile and laugh because it makes her smile back occasionally. I want to sleep.

And so here I am. Typing this. Feeling overwhelmingly

...Guilty.

November 25

It Takes A Village

When you have a baby, you very quickly get over being embarrassed or conservative about many things. The words breasts, nipples and poo suddenly become as frequently used as the words coffee, chocolate and sleep. As a breastfeeding mum, you have to get over the weirdness of pulling your boobs out anywhere and everywhere because if you didn't, you would never leave your bedroom, and neither would your baby. As a mum with a new baby, you find yourself being asked by perfect strangers about breastfeeding. Are you breastfeeding? How's it going? Why are you doing/not-doing A/B/C? As though it is somehow their business, and it isn't weird to be discussing your nipples with your hairdresser. And if, like me, anything is out of the normal, then be prepared to explain it to everyone.

I am having to use nipple shields to feed my baby. Now to me, the fact that I am breastfeeding her at all is a miracle. I have inverted nipples—the worst my lactation consultant has ever seen apparently—and this means that there is nothing for baby to latch on to. The shields give her the ability to latch, and therefore the ability to feed. Getting this going was a mission and I almost gave up completely at weeks 2, 3 and 6. In fact, a number of midwives, psychologists and even my lactation consultant actually suggested that perhaps I should consider switching to formula to avoid becoming incredibly overwhelmed and depressed. However, I am notoriously stubborn. If my mum could do it, so could I. By week 7, I went for 24 hours without using a bottle of formula, expressed milk or pumping, and I was absolutely elated!

Since then I've been relatively successful, only feeding her formula a handful of times when she was out with her Dad, or on the one night that I went out with my friends. Success! I am incredibly proud of this achievement, as I was convinced it was going to be impossible for me to breastfeed at all, yet here I am. Of course, whenever I pull out the shields, everyone wants to know why. So the secret shame I harboured for most of my life, is now known to all and sundry.

Which is why, as I am now forced to consider mixed feeding in order to regain my sanity, I am feeling incredibly, overwhelmingly conflicted. Last night I lost it. I had a complete meltdown. I felt so angry and so frustrated and at my wits end in every sense of the word. I couldn't think straight, I could barely see straight. After 11 weeks of being woken every 1-3 hours for feeding, I'm finally wondering if all those people weren't right from the start. Clearly I am not able to hack the sleep deprivation that goes hand-in-hand with exclusively breastfeeding. I am angry with my Husband for being able to go to work, for going for an hour run once a week, for not being able to find the debit card that was in my bag, for letting her fall asleep on him every night, even though I do that during the day, for not being home with me during the day to help me. I can see how people get to the point of wanting to shake their babies, as though that is somehow going to snap them into consciousness and make them realise that if they just went to sleep, everything would be easier.

Which of course, is ridiculous. She's just 11 weeks old. She is only crying because she is so overtired she can't fall asleep anymore. And Husband needs to go to work, otherwise we wouldn't be able to afford to live, eat or do anything remotely fun. His runs aren't a way for him to make me feel more isolated, they are helping keep him sane. Which is a good thing. At least one of us needs to be. I know that all I need to do is say the word, and I too could go have some time to myself. Only, at the moment I feel that this is impossible because I am exclusively breastfeeding. I can't leave her in case she gets hungry, I can't have a few hours in the afternoon or evening where I go out because if she has a bottle of formula, it will mess up my supply and I will feel an intense sense of failure. And so here I am, considering mixed feeding and feeling guilty about it because, "Breast is best", "Formula isn't natural" and "Why aren't you breastfeeding your baby?" But what about "Happy wife, happy life", "Baby needs a coherent mum", "Don't be a mombie" (Mom + Zombie) and "Sleep deprivation is your biggest trigger for depression"?

It takes a village to raise a child. Little Bean deserves to have a Mum who isn't crying constantly, or wanting to hit her father, or feeling hard done by and exhausted. She deserves to feel loved. To be happy and to *see* happy. I can't do that alone. If giving her a bottle of formula once or twice a day and sharing the feeds so that I can get an hour more sleep is what it takes to remain sane, how is that any worse than her Dad spending an hour less time with her so that he can go for a run to maintain his sanity? It takes a village to keep the parents sane. To give them time to find themselves again, to spend time together, and to exit the baby haze once in a while. It takes a village to look out for them and make sure they are ok. Last night J rang me at 10 pm after I texted her saying I wanted to walk out. It took 20 minutes, but she managed to calm me down enough to want to apologise to my Husband. This morning, A came round after reading the text I sent her last night, to help me get some rest and to vent a bit. She is currently in the nursery trying to settle Baby for the third time. On the weekend my whole family arrived out of nowhere, and suddenly my house was clean, and I was able to go get my hair done and have some down time. My parents even left dinner in the fridge so we didn't have to cook that night. I only wish we lived closer to some family so that we could remain saner for longer.

I guess I have to work at building my own village family in order to make up for the fact that we live so far from our real ones. And this pressure on mums about breastfeeding needs to end. Yes, it's wonderful and it is the best food for baby, but the mum's need looking after too. It takes a village to remind a Mum to do that. And all too often, in this age of being constantly connected, we are left alone.

December 11

My Bald Baby

My Baby Girl has a lot of hair.

Good. Now that that's out of the way I feel I can move on with my life.

No!

Apparently I CANNOT move on with my life. Nope, not until I have been alerted to the unusual amount of hair on her head by, oh I don't know, how about: Every. Single. Person.

Here are some things people have suggested I say, as a way to make it more interesting for myself.

Typical interaction.

Stranger/acquaintance: "Look at all that hair!"

Me: "Yes, she does have rather a lot."

<u>**Suggested interactions.**</u>

Stranger/acquaintance: "Look at all that hair!"

Me: "It's a wig."

Stranger/acquaintance: "Look at all that hair!"

Me: "Yeah, can't wait for it to get a bit longer so I can cut it into a mullet to match her daddy. At least, we think that's her daddy, the other guy was bald so..."

Stranger/acquaintance: "Look at all that hair!"

Me: "Really? Oh, now that you mention it..."

Stranger/acquaintance: "Look at all that hair!"

Me: "What? OMG THAT'S NOT MY BABY!"

So yes, my 13-week-old Little Bean looks like a tiny adult already, and receives an awful lot of attention. I've managed to master the art of keeping moving and nodding politely whilst muttering a Harry Potter death curse under my breath, but some women (and yes it is almost always women), are unseemingly persistent. Apparently blind to the unfriendly (and often downright hostile) body language, and deaf to the not so subtle tones of, "Leave me alone."

December 20

Learning

Recently a blog has been circulating my Facebook circle, regarding what are good presents for childless people to buy for their friend's kids, and what are not. As I read it, I found myself nodding my head at every single item...both because I had received these items and understood why not to give them, and also (strangely) because only months ago, I myself had gifted these exact items to friends with all the best of intentions. CRAZY!

As we are now in the final two weeks of the year 2013, I find myself reflecting back on what an intense year it has been for our little family, and at the same time, suddenly realising just how much I have changed and learnt during the course of it. So, in typical me fashion, I figured I'd blog about it!

The 2013 List of Things I Learnt About...

...BABY CLOTHES

The cuter the outfit, the less likely it is to be worn.

This goes for both baby and mum. Cute cotton baby dresses with frilly bits and gorgeous buttons that go UP THE BACK??? May look to-die-for on the rack, and believe me, you would rather die than attempt to put that on a baby and then have them wear it for a day. They end up under their armpits for the most part, nappies on display all day, buttons up the back are a nightmare to do on a baby that can't even sit up yet, let alone undoing them for the numerous changes you WILL have to endure because of spit up, leaking nappies, or just general wetness. Give me a onesie that has domes ONLY on the crotch, and is made of jersey fabric any day over a dress. Shove some cute pants over it, put on some socks and tuck those pants into the socks and you're set!

...PREGNANCY

It Sucks.

Even now, I am often confronted by Mums who say things like, "Don't you wish you could be pregnant again, just so you can have a break?"

Honestly? No. No, I do not. Pregnancy was painful, gross, tiring and just awful in every way. There was literally nothing I enjoyed about being pregnant. But there is plenty I like about being a Mum.

...CHILDBIRTH

Was a breeze compared to what came after.

You recall how I spent all that time freaking out about labour during the year? Well, mummies, I have learnt my lesson. Labour was awful, excruciating and terrifying, but at least it was definitely going to end, and with the epidural, I even managed to escape it for a while. The weeks immediately after giving birth are far, far worse. Physically, mentally, and emotionally extreme. In fact, I would do labour all over again if it meant I was spared those first few weeks....well the lack of sleep bits anyway. Which incidentally, is the majority of it.

...THE MUMMY CLUB CONSPIRACY

Those happy mums and gorgeous photos of happy families on Facebook—It's only a glimpse of reality.

Sure, that status may say they are "so in love", and that picture of the smiling baby is "so adorable". But that's only half the truth. Yes, they love the baby, but that doesn't mean they always like the baby. You try 'liking' a crying baby at 3 am when you have literally done everything you can think of to calm them, and you haven't slept in 20 hours. Most parents only post the good times. Which in turn adds to the general opinion of childless people that babies are always awesome, and being a parent is easy.

...SLEEP

I can survive on much less than I ever thought possible.

I remember the days where I got eight hours.....IN A ROW!!
Cue manic laughter

I have nothing more to say on that topic.

...MY BABY

Is the most awesome thing that has ever happened to me. EVER.

Sure, I don't get much sleep, and I usually am only guessing at what she is wanting. But recently she has started having these awesome baby conversations with me, and smiling these amazing smiles. I think she really likes me! Which makes my heart glow brighter. I never get tired of her smiles, and I am so excited to know what her laugh sounds like, whether she's left or right handed, what her favourite food is, what song does she like the most, what does she sound like when she talks.....The future is a veritable feast of new discoveries and I can't wait.

December 20

A Christmas Letter

Dear Little Bean,

This will be your first Christmas ever, and we are so excited. We haven't got you a present, as we don't think you'd really care, and we should probably save that money for a high chair as you are growing and learning SO fast, that we almost can't keep up! This time last year you were a thought in my head, an idea that sparked such excitement in me that I was already starting to dream about you. I knew you were there before I even found out I was pregnant because I dreamt about you. I asked you what we should call my mum, and you said, "Nana Ali." In my dream I said, "A-, That's a great name," and when I rang Nana Ali the next day to tell her, she said, "That's funny, 'cos that's the exact name I came up with yesterday."

We've had a rough start you and I. I wish I could do the beginning of your life all over again and make it better for both of us. I would tell the delivery theatre doctors to leave you be, to not take you away from me the minute you were born. I would hold you and tell them to leave you alone. I would figure out a way to stay by your side in the NICU ward, and I wouldn't let them tell me to not stroke your tiny hand. But I can't. So instead I am focusing on making your future the best that I can.

I wish I could protect you from all that the world is going to throw at you. I wish I could keep you hidden from its horrors forever. I wish that I could guarantee that you will never have to feel the pain of a schoolyard fist, or the sting of a bullying remark, or the ache of a broken heart. I pray that you don't feel the same anxiety I did as a teenager or have the same battle with depression. I hope that I can be the role model you need me to be in order to become strong enough to deal with life's struggles. But I can't promise any of that. All I can do is promise that I will be there with you for it all. I will catch you when you fall and I will always pick you back up. I only hope I can give you the life you deserve.

Little Bean, you have changed me in ways I can't even describe. I used to be anxious all the time about what people thought of me, about death and pain, about me failing. But that changed the moment you were born. I still worry about what people think of me, but I care less about it. I don't freak out about performing because I want to show you that I am not scared and neither should you be. I fear death only because I am worried about what will happen to you if I am not around, and rather than worry that I will fail and embarrass myself, I worry that I will fail you most of all.

This Christmas you are nearly four months old. You smile and coo, and are about to laugh any day now. You are just learning to roll over and to grasp at toys. You still wake 2-3 times a night and you don't like to sleep in your cot during the day. You love bath time and you love singing with Daddy and I. I don't know what the future holds for us, but I do know that I will love you for every single second of it. Probably you won't read this letter for many, many years, but when you do, believe me when I say that all this will still be true.

I Love You,

Mum.

Author's Note

Becoming Mum began as a way to process what was going on for me as a regular blog. I've always kept a diary, so I guess that writing is a way I can really figure things out. I definitely make more sense written down than I if I just speak!

I never intended it to end up as a book. I actually had no plans for it at all. All I thought was I need to know I'm not alone in this, so I'll write about it and then perhaps someone else read it and feel less alone themselves. That was literally all I was thinking.

It turned into something much bigger than that, and as the year went on, it was clear that many people were being affected by what I was writing in many different ways. My family for one, started talking to each other in ways they hadn't before, and suddenly I was in communication with relations I hadn't really talked to since I was a teenager.

Stories were told that hadn't been told before, and bit-by-bit, I found myself discovering things about myself that made far more sense than they ever had before. My anxiety hasn't come out of nowhere, I'm not the first in my family to have a panic attack or be depressed, and we all struggled with breastfeeding and hated being pregnant.

It's amazing what a little openness can do, if you share your story, others will share theirs with you and you will realise you are not alone at all. Asking for help may be hard, but people will always respond and there is always someone you know who has had a similar experience.

So whether you are pregnant, have children, or are thinking about trying, I hope this book has given you some laughs and encouragement. Becoming 'Mum' is both the worst and best experience in the world. But as the clichés state all too truthfully, each moment will pass all too soon, and it really is all worth it.

Babydust!

Follow my continuing journey at:

anxietygirlgetspregnant.blogspot.co.nz

Services I Used Along the way

Mothers Matter (Christchurch)

This is a Post-Natal Depression support group in Christchurch, NZ. They are an invaluable resource for mothers who are struggling with depression and anxiety post birth and have no age limit on the children. The meetings are really well set up, with tea, coffee and lovely volunteers who look after the kids for two hours so that the mothers can talk without feeling like they are talking 'bad' in front of their kids, or being constantly interrupted.

In order to run they need to have funding approved every year, and unfortunately, this year it wasn't approved. If you feel like donating to help it keep providing the service, please contact Sonya Watson through the Mothers Matter Facebook page.

Similarly, if you or someone you know might benefit from a little support, have a look at their website. It has a wealth of information about mental illness, medications and services available nationwide for women to make use of pre, post and during pregnancy.

www.mothersmatter.co.nz

Anxiety Disorders Unit (ADU) (Christchurch)

I've been through this service a couple of times now, and they are fantastic. They offer one on one psychiatric treatment and intensive group therapy free of charge. You must get referred by your doctor and unfortunately, there is a very long waiting list in order to get seen. But once you do get it, it is worth it. Thank you to Monique and Jenny who really helped me out.

Mothers and Babies Unit (Christchurch)

This is a specialized mental health service for mothers (and fathers) who are experiencing mental health issues while pregnant and for the first year post natal. The wait is less than the ADU and they are able to make home visits and hospital visits. Which, believe me, is a godsend when you have a newborn. They also have an inpatient service for those who are really struggling.

Plunket Post Natal Adjustment Program (PNAP) (Nationwide)

For mothers and fathers who are struggling with depression and anxiety on a mild to moderate level. Free of charge, and offering ongoing support for those who aren't struggling enough to need more specialised help through the Mothers and Babies service. Just call the number in your area for more information. All details are available on the plunket website.

Remember, the services are there for you to use. So use them! People want to help you. So let them!

Hang in there,
Jess

www.ingramcontent.com/pod-product-compliance
Ingram Content Group UK Ltd.
Pitfield, Milton Keynes, MK11 3LW, UK
UKHW020241250726
13967UKWH00001B/496

9 781312 029743